Stage set of the Llaregyb Players in Under Milk Wood, Laugharne, 1958.
Preliminary pencil drawing for a large oil painting.

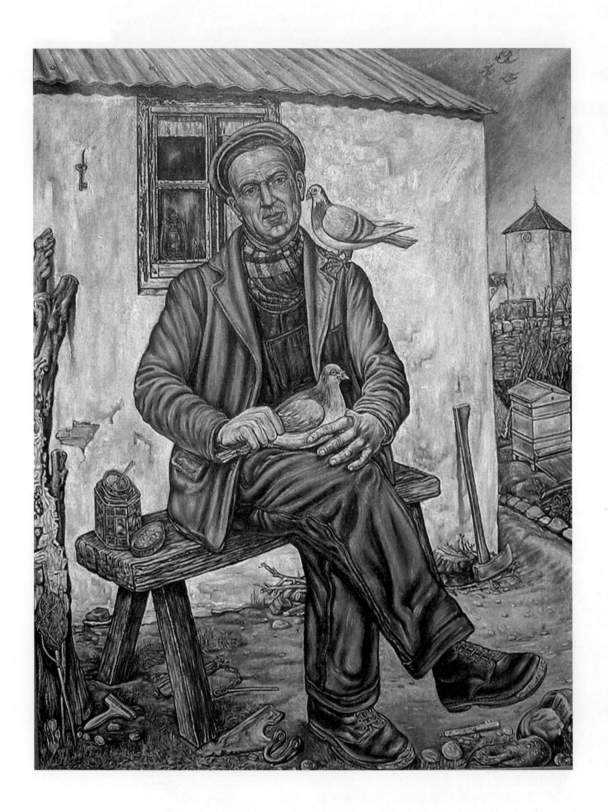

Mr Coles, the Pidgeon Man of Llanybri - see page 102

LAUGHARNE AND DYLAN THOMAS

My late wife, Min Lewis, first wrote the original version of "Laugharne and Dylan Thomas" in 1963 and it was published in 1967, and dedicated it to Dylan's memory. She always longed to see a new and enlarged edition, with extra illustrations to elucidate her text, and with this in mind, my daughter, Jennifer Heywood and I set about this task. I would like to express my sincere thanks to Jennifer for her unstinting support and effort in helping to bring Min's wish to fruition, without which this publication would not have been possible.

Min and I lived in Laugharne for many years, during which time I was the principal at the Carmarthen School of Art and it was whilst living there that these additional illustrations were created.

I therefore wish to dedicate this revised and superior edition to Min,
my dear departed wife and best friend of sixty years.

Stanley Lewis

Also
I wish to thank the following people for all their help and
support during the production of this 2nd Edition.
Graham C. Barr, Managing Director of Taylor & Clifton Ltd.
Dr. Patrick Oates, Art Historian
Roger Cucksey, Keeper (Art) - Newport South Wales
Ron Williams, Friend and local Saddleworth Poet
Di and Tony Howard, Travel Writers and Photographers
Bev Heywood, my son-in-law

LAUGHARNE AND DYLAN THOMAS

by

Min Lewis

Illustrated by Stanley Lewis

Min and Stanley Lewis share with Dylan Thomas not only their Welsh ancestry and upbringing, but also their love of Laugharne as their adopted home. Laugharne was, indeed, one of Dylan Thomas's favourite places. He worked and lived here, and very few would ever have heard of this quiet place near Carmarthen in Wales had it not been for him.

Like Thomas, Min and Stanley Lewis came to visit and were captivated by this unique, proud, self-contained town whose history, customs, people and associations are affectionately and humorously presented in LAUGHARNE AND DYLAN THOMAS.

The author and her husband, whose line illustrations accompany the text, knew Dylan Thomas as a private person, at home and relaxed among people who regarded him as one of themselves and judged him as such. This judgement reveals a man well-contrasted to many of the over-dramatized portrayals by those who knew him only on the public stage.

This book is unique in that it is the first to be written about Dylan Thomas by a resident of Laugharne where he was so much at home, and it contains many anecdotes contributed by local people who met and knew him as those who viewed him from a distance could not. Many of these contributors will be present at the party to be held to mark the publication of LAUGHARNE AND DYLAN THOMAS at Brown's Hotel, Laugharne at 12 noon on Tuesday 1st August 1967. The room will be decorated with Stanley Lewis's illustrations for the book.

The township of Laugharne is the last surviving example of a mediaeval corporation still retaining its ancient customs and tradit-ions. These rights were granted to the burgesses of Laugharne by Charter in the reign of Edward I. It is the scene of a triennial Dylan Thomas Festival which this year is being held from 1st - 5th August, 1967. Performances of UNDER MILK WOOD (DAN Y WENALLT) are being presented at the Glan-y-Mor Theatre, Laugharne each night, except Wednesday, and on Saturday afternoon. The performances on Friday evening 4th August and Saturday afternoon 5th August will be in Welsh.

LAUGHARNE AND DYLAN THOMAS is published, to coincide with the Festival this year, by Dennis Dobson, 80 Kensington Church Street, London W.8., at 45s 0d net.

This is a 1967 leaflet advertising the launching of Laugharne & Dylan Thomas by Min Lewis at Brown's Hotel on 1st August 1967

Dylan's Vintage Town
by
Min Lewis - *Upton House*
Laugharne, Carmarthenshire - 1961

Laugharne, pronounced Larne, a small town in Carmarthenshire, in South West Wales, rich in antiquity.

One hundred and fifty years ago, it was described as a remarkable place, though out of the route of the general traveller, remote from the bustle of the world, from those hives of industry and those thorough-fares which lead to them or even to a great city, in fact, no thorough-fare at all; persons from most distant parts of the world find it out somehow, and make it either their home or a temporary resting place, but they soon discover there is no place where things will be more quickly known and their affairs thoroughly investigated, no place where kinder people are found, no place where good nature has been more abused. The climate though not bracing, is healthy, beneficial to persons with delicate lungs. The air most salubrious and health giving, tending to lengthen life.

Just over one hundred and fifty years ago, it was the custom to hang the heads of foxes, badgers, pole cats, wild cats, and owls on a yew tree near the Church door in the South transept called the 'Fox Tree'. After the heads had hung for three church services a reward was given.

In the register of Laugharne church is this account, dated May 5th 1723:

'For every vixen fox 6d, dog fox 1/-, cub or young fox of either sex under one year old, 1/-, every badger 6d, wild cat 6d, owl 3d. Signed Thomas Phillips, vicar.'

Many inns about Laugharne were kept by bad characters who murdered innocent travellers for money and jewelery.

One particularly bad house, notorious for murdering travellers, was the 'Three Lords Inn', no longer an inn, but an innocent small farm.

Travellers were put into a very large oven, so contrived that they fell into a dungeon beneath. The roads of Laugharne were infested with robbers.

Welsh superstition was strong, they believed that lights traversed the road by which the dead would be carried to burial.

The light was supposed to appear in answer to the prayer of St Lanon, who desired that people be warned before death came, and so prepare themselves. It is recorded in the 'Antiquities of Laugharne', by Mary Curtis: May 24th 1880. 'A husband was very near his end, when his wife said to him, "There is a curious light on the Strand, what can it be?" He replied, "It is the light before death, it is for me." Soon afterwards he died.'

Laugharne would not be complete without a ghost, and Gosport House, an ancient resident has a 'White Lady'.

Two young boys, the sons of a family living in it 150 years ago, used to see every night after they were in bed, the appearance of a woman passing across the window, her figure enveloped in drapery, her hands covering her face, as though in distress of mind, or in deep devotion.

It was at the window of the room over the drawing room looking on to the sea.

The architecture of Laugharne has changed little in 150 years, the names are the same, Cock Shelly, Ants Hill, Horse Pool, Stony Way, Fern Hill, White Spot; and the houses and farms have enchanting names like, Salt House, Honey Cors, Island House, Upper Marsh, Old Malt House, Witchett, Little Burrows, The Gin Shop, Beacons Hill, and many more.

Bull baiting and cock fighting were discontinued 150 years ago.

What picture does Laugharne conjure up in 1961? 'Up street with the toffs, down street with the toughs' and along the up and down street, an ancient town hall with a gold weather cock that turns with the wind; dignified Queen Ann houses, some elegantly tall, some dwarfish short, a tumble down castle with a rakish history, cockles, curlews, a church enshrined with dark mysterious yews and cracked tomb stones, lime washed cottages and cobble street, and along the cliff walk, where the banks are draped with old man's beard and hawthorn berries, the tucked away, hush-a-bye house of Dylan Thomas.

The windows have a vacant glare, the door is blue with cold, a dangerously narrow cliff pathway cries "Look out, beware," and below a sheer drop of sandstone rock, where pink and white plants flourish; the lapping waves lick the stones.

Sometimes a mysterious greyness hides the green patch work hills across the river, it is still, and peaceful except for the cries of curlews, screeching gulls, and cormorants; and when the day is clear, a heron can be seen fishing in the pools, hunting flat fish in the sandy mud. Sometimes a boat bobs on the restless, moving water, sometimes a stranger with a camera will try to capture the mysterious mellow beauty, and look enraptured at the small cottage Boat House, and see 'Sir John's Hill', and hear a hundred, nay a thousand voices cry out:

"This is Laugharne," for this is surely Laugharne, and this was Dylan's home.

The nearest neighbour, a modernised beyond recognition Ferry house, once an inn, a white washed cottage with bull's eye glass windows standing perilously near the water's edge, where a family of boatmen brothers ran the ferry between the over river hills of Llanstephan where the ruined bell house remains, to the whispering, never to be spoken aloud, township of Laugharne.

The old Ferry house where for years the nephew of the boatmen, a deaf mute, lived alone, until an elderly woman was murdered up street, and he was the suspect. They called him Budha, but he was no god, neither was he proved a murderer, so now he lives his silent life in an institution; the murder remains unsolved.

Follow the mud path into the moist wood, Milkwood, perhaps, inhale the rotting leaf mould, admire the delicate fern growing from damp moss covered trunks of trees, and the banks of primroses in spring.

Look down the steep sloping tree infested bank to the grass patch that was once a tennis court for ladies in straw boaters and Edwardian dresses of the great house above; where peacocks once strutted on well kept lawns, and magnolia trees still grace the front, the stables are dying with decay.

See to the right the burnt out shell of a well proportioned house, where trees grow from the walls, the wind whines eerily like voices of the past, 'Gone, gone, gone for ever.'

The mud pathway leads on to the meadows, lush pasture where foxes play in spinneys, and live in overgrown banks; but we are leaving Laugharne behind, so return once more to the cliff, past the Ferry and Dylan's home to the main King street, so called because Henry 2nd King of England, came to Laugharne in 1171; with Brown's hotel that is not an hotel, just an ordinary 'Come to drink' pub, and opposite the tall 'Pelican', once an inn, now a private house where Dylan's mother lived for a time, and was reputed to remark when bed-ridden, and could see from her window, Dylan going into the Brown's, "I see him going in, oh that I could see him coming out." But it was always dark.

Dylan was not an alcoholic, he drank beer in the old musty pubs of Laugharne to listen to old men's tales, and barmaids' gossip, which he usually scribbled down on empty cigarette packets. He never aired his views, just listened like the dreamer that he was.

On his first visit to America, he left instruction with the local grocer shopkeeper, to supply his wife with whatever food she and the family required, and he would 'settle up' on his return.

"Which he did," related the shopkeeper, "by pulling out of his pocket bundles of notes, and telling me to take what was owing", and quite surprised the shopkeeper added, "He didn't even look at the bill."

The amateur Llaregyb Players of Carmarthenshire performed his most controversial work "Under Milkwood" in Laugharne in 1958 for the first time. It was enacted in a marquee pitched at Dragon's Park, which was neither a park, nor a dragon, but just a flat field belonging to the farm of that name. The canvas marquee was expensive to hire, and although the Players performed to a full house, they lost money, fortunately it was supported by the Carmarthenshire Community Council. It ran for five performances, after each performance the Players, who had strong Welsh voices, would congregate at the 'Cross House' inn for a typical Welsh sing-song, reviving ancient hymns and Welsh folk songs with great gusto and hwyl, (Welsh term for receiving the spirit).

Dylan's mother lived at the Boat House then, and she was delighted to meet and encourage the Players.

The producer decided to hold a party after the last performance on the Saturday night in the marquee. Everyone looked forward with expectation to tots of whisky, rum, gin, intellectual talk and of course good singing, every one was in good spirit; but as the voices of the last performance of 'Under Milkwood' faded, Dylan's mother passed peacefully away, a sad end to a happy week, and there was no party that night, for no one was in party mood.

In the spring the cherry trees are shrouded in a profusion of pink blossom, it is the time when strangers visit Laugharne, and ask to see Dylan's house and Dylan's grave, they pass a graveyard on the way to the cliff overlooking the bay, where once a Welsh chapel stood, the pulpit is now part of the counter of Brown's hotel, the chapel is no more, but the grey stones remain in untidy assortment.

The people of Laugharne do not notice strangers much, they come and go like rain, and are thought no more of. They all knew Dylan by sight, few knew him intimately, many wondered whether he had caricatured them in Under Milkwood, whether Laugharne was in fact Under Milkwood; but Laugharne like any other Welsh village has its Mrs Dai Bread 1, Mrs Dai Bread 2, Eli Jenkins the minister, and of course the luscious 'come to bed' Polly Carter.

There is surprise when Americans come to Laugharne, "All Americans are millionaires," they think, "He is thought a lot of in America", they say, but perhaps a prophet is never acknowledged in his own town.

So days come, and days go, and Laugharne only alters with the seasons. She is a blossoming bride in spring, a full bloomed wife in summer, ages slightly in autumn, shivers with grey mists and cold winds in winter, and all the time the sea birds chatter and make love, the tide comes in, and goes out, and Dylan's house stands calmly on the buttock of the cliff, sees all, hears all, and says nothing.

So the years come and go, and this year the Llaregyb Players returned to perform 'Under Milkwood' for the second time, and pitched their canvas marquee on a high hill where the wind and rain lashed with unceasing fury, and tore the canvas in two, so that one performance did not go on.

People wondered why we called the week 'Laugharne Festival' and not 'Dylan's Week', but it was agreed that we would get more local support if it was called 'Laugharne Festival', Why? There are still some local people who almost spit on the ground at Dylan's name, but they are the minority.

Strangers were shocked at the state of his grave, but unkempt and weed ridden with a simple cross, it stood out a mile amongst the other marble monstrosities. Reporters from National newspapers flocked to Laugharne to ask why. Why was his grave neglected? Why only a wooden cross? Why the indifference of the Laugharne people to Wales' greatest poet? Was it true that 50% of the Laugharne people that were for Dylan were the boozers? I say "No," 25% of the people are for Dylan, the other 75% merely indifferent, but their indifference gives Laugharne a magical charm. There are no knick-knack shops selling souvenirs, the only souvenirs for sale are the books he wrote clearly marked, 'A Prospect of the Sea' by Dylan Thomas, 'Quite Early One Morning' by Dylan Thomas and of course 'Under Milkwood'.

The ugly signs strung along the cliff bearing the words, 'Dylan's Walk' have been mercifully torn down, for I am sure the only sign Dylan would have appreciated would have been 'The Ferry Inn', for Dylan wrote of Laugharne: "They envy Laugharne its minding of its own, strange business, its same disregard for haste, its generous acceptance of the follies of others having so many, ripe and piping of its own, its insular, featherbed air, its philosophy of "It will all be the same in a hundred years time". They deplore its right to be in their eyes so wrong, and to enjoy it so much as well, and, through envy and indignation they label and libel it a legendary lazy little black-magical bedlam by the sea. And is it? Of course not, I hope.

After a Welsh newspaper devoted a page of photography to Dylan's grave, with a broken vase holding a few wild flowers, many visitors arrived to investigate. But I believe that people should come to Laugharne because they admire Dylan's work, not merely to see where a cross marks the spot.

So when you mention Dylan in Laugharne, people at once curse the American writer John Brinnin for his misleading description of "Dylan in America', for this was not the Dylan they knew, his fellow drinkers say:

"Dylan was a beer drinker, that Brinnin was a liar," and "If he comes to Laugharne we will run him out of town." Women? Dylan had no affair with any woman in Laugharne, "He was not much for women," says the locals, and they should know, for weren't Dylan's most productive years spent in Laugharne?

Other writers have lived here, Richard Hughes, author of 'High Wind in Jamaica', and his latest, 'The Fox in the Attic' rented the house attached to the castle. Augustus John the Welsh painter who stayed at the castle and first introduced Dylan to Caitlin, once stayed at the Brown's hotel with his wife Dorelia, only to be thrown out in the early hours of the morning by the landlord who had drunk too much.

An assortment of writers stay periodically at the Boat House, life in Laugharne is never dull. There is a ninety five year old man living alone, who walks the steep hill from down street to up street each day to shop, he lived in Russia for twenty years and boasts that he installed electricity in the Kremlin; he left on the outbreak of the revolution, and has lived in Laugharne ever since, and there is a Portreeve, an ancient charter, burgess', and Laugharne is the smallest town in Great Britain.

So if you sit as I often do, on the wooden seat on the cliff on which the art of cutting out letters has been practised until it looks like a jumbled alphabet, you will see the old man's beard draping the hedges like detergent foam, the silvery sparkling water, and blue mist of distant hills, feel the warmth of the autumn sun, see the gulls in a cloudless sky, and the distant mountainous sand dunes tipped with wiry grass, a fig tree in Dylan's garden that bears uneatable figs, the first red berries of holly, a grass snake sunning itself on a bed of violet leaves, intermingled with ivy, herb robert, bramble, wild strawberry and briar. The distant Welsh farm, virginal white, crouched like a prisoner on the belly of the hill, and listen spell bound to the cries of curlews, gulls and cormorants.

A week has passed and gale force winds have stripped the trees of leaves, it is still warm on the sheltered cliff, and the rippling, murmuring water, is slowly filling up the sand banks, the birds wait in hopeful anticipation, "Fish, fish," they cry, "Flat fish in the mudbanks, prawns in the pools, cockles lying snugly in beds," waiting, hunting, eating, living.

Mountainous cotton wool clouds float aimlessly across the blue sky, changing constantly into abstract patterns, yet all is not peaceful in the small town of Laugharne, a storm rages as a speculative opportunist threatens the unspoilt countryside with a caravan site. Carmarthen Town and Country planning say "No", the county council say "No", the District rural council say "No", Laugharne Corporation say "No", but he has gone above the heads of all to far away London, and her Majesty's Inspector came to Laugharne to hear the case at an open meeting.

How we fought and squabbled in the unheated hall, as the wind raged, hail stones beat down, thunder crashed and drowned the voices.

Merlin the famous enchanter of the legends connected with King Arthur, wrote:

"Kidwelli was, Carmarthen is, and Laugharne will be, the greatest city of the three."

Have we won the fight to keep Laugharne the unspoilt jewel that it is? For Dylans's sake I hope so.

End

Derek Gardner 13d Sheffield Terrace Kensington Church Street London W8 Park 3210

21st September, 1967

Mrs. A.M.O'Toole,
Brown's Hotel,
Laugharne,
Wales.

Dear Mrs. O'Toole,

Now that I have returned to London, I have had an opportunity of discussing your bill for the party held on August 1st, not only with Mrs. Lewis but also with the publishers, who are making a contribution towards the cost. I must confess that we are all agreed that the account rendered of £140 seems rather high if not excessive.

Let me say at once that there is, of course, no dispute over the charge for the champagne and it would, of course, have been far easier to see how your account was made out if a more detailed statement had been given showing costs of food ordered etc.   I understand from Mrs. Lewis that she herself bought two salmon but it is, of course, realised that these were cooked by you and that a considerable quantity of other food, including turkeys, was purchased by you.

Furthermore, I am sure you will be the first to appreciate that a very considerable amount of voluntary help was given by several people in connection with the preparation of the ballroom for the party and in the preparing and serving of the food and drink.

I am sorry to have to write this letter but, as you know, I have a responsibility both to Mrs. Lewis and the publishers in this matter.   I am sure that a reasonable and amicable settlement can be arranged, but in the first instance I would ask you to be kind enough to send me a more detailed account.

I am sending a copy of this letter to Mrs. Lewis, whom you will no doubt be seeing, and in the meantime have forwarded your account in respect of Mr. and Mrs. Blake to the publishers, who will be responsible for this.

Yours sincerely,

Derek Gardner

Min's literary agent queries the launching bill of Brown's Hotel.

Foreword
by Aeronwy Thomas

As is made clear by the book's title, "Laugharne and Dylan Thomas" the subject is Laugharne and its links with my father, Dylan Thomas. I am lucky enough to have a copy of the original book which was launched in 1967 in the convivial atmosphere of Brown's Hotel. Doubtless, many of the characters identified by the authoress, Min Lewis, as sources for the play for voices, Under Milk Wood, were present.

One such character translated into the haberdasher Mog Edwards for the radio play written by my father while living in Laugharne was Mr Watts. I can remember him in my childhood, selling corsets and other items which he could sell unlike the radio character who complained that business was "poorly". In this new book, other sources for "Under Milk Wood" have been identified such as a local called Johnny Holloway, possibly the inspiration for Captain Cat.

In effect, approximately seventy new illustrations (including the captain) and photographs have been added to this splendid new edition. Min Lewis's husband, Stanley Lewis (now nearly a hundred years old), and the original illustrator, has released other work not used at the time.

I am very excited by the publication of such a book with its new material lovingly gathered and collated by the Lewis's daughter, Jennifer Heywood, containing unseen letters and articles of local and general interest. The only sadness is that Min Lewis, whom I remember as an ardent fan of my father's works and a friend, cannot be here to enjoy the republication and extended edition of this book.

Meantime, my very best wishes to all involved in such a splendid and worthwhile project.

Aeronwy

Aeronwy Thomas

Foreword

This remarkable historical reference book was originally published thirty six years ago in 1967 as a result of the creative and incisive energies of Stanley Cornwell Lewis A.R.C.A., Artist and Illustrator, and his late wife, the Writer of Childrens' Books and Literary Reviewer, Min Lewis. Subsequently its unique treatment of combining Stanley's period drawings and Min's literary style and text came to assure and confirm, in an unintended act of scholarship, much of the social context in which Dylan Thomas clarified his impassioned observations as he revealed his sensitive poetic themes. It is within this new and retrospective scholarship that the qualities of this Edition should be appraised and re-assessed, particularly since Dylan's work is now currently enjoying such a positive re-evaluation and review, fifty years after his death.

The collection of Drawings and Writings this edition contains came about as a result of a personal friendship between Stanley and Min Lewis with Dylan and Caitlin Thomas, during the years of their association with Laugharne in South Wales. The lives and times; landscapes and personalities they witnessed, and mutually embraced in that small post-war community, came to define Dylan's great and evocative work, 'Under Milkwood'.

As a historical study, this volume provides the reader with the closest possible authentic reference to the complete social characteristic and stylistic period setting of the times; enabling a true interaction with Dylan's infamous personalities and familiar places as he *would have seen and known them*. To read the text and assimilate the illustrations in this book in parallel to 'Milkwood', will enrich the reader's pleasure and insight, by creating a real sense of original 'place' within the theatricism of Dylan's imagined dramas, stagecraft and setting.

Much has been explored and chronicled about the life and times of Dylan Thomas, of his genius, his raw exposure to hedonistic societies, with their distracting appetites; of his complex relationships, and the circumstances affecting his turbulent life and its attendant tragic decline. What is also known, is that his formative years in South Wales, in the earlier part of the last century gave voice to his phenomenal imagination, and forged the poetic irony in the way he defined and embellished the principal characters of his work.

Stanley Lewis is a child of those times too. Originally from Newport in South Wales, he was born in 1905. As a child, he was prodigally gifted as an instinctive and intuitive artist, with an exceptional ability in visual recollection and a compulsion to draw. His mother was deeply sensitive to his abilities, and his father too; but taking a more practical view of matters, it was his father that encouraged Stanley to train to be an Architect, and he did join an architectural practice for a time, but:

"I couldn't cope with all that surveying, number working and trigonometry"

In recent times, at the age of 98 years, he has moved to Saddleworth in Yorkshire Northern England following his wife's death in January 2003. Yet his vitality and clarity of anecdotal detail has not left him; he still draws and reworks many of his early studies, in a marvellously chaotic new Pennine studio overlooking Saddleworth Moor, surrounded by thousands of his books, drawings and paintings. Indeed, all the original drawings in this book are still within this archive alongside some seventy five additional works intended, but omitted, for inclusion in the First Edition. As a consequence of his active participation in this project, some forty years on, he now regards this book as the definitive *'Revised First Edition'*, and it is of special note that he regards these additional works as having a particular resonance with Min's original refreshing and unabridged texts.

Stanley thrives on new projects and is completely contemporary in his intellectual grasp of the History of Art and Artists of his acquaintance. He recalls with great affection his dear friend the late Arnold Haskell, Principal of the Royal School of Ballet, with whom he and Min became involved in a Museum of Victorian Child Memorabilia, in Bath, and also the astonishing collection of 'Impressionist' paintings and Rodin drawings that Haskell had put together. Jacob Epstein, the great figurative Sculptor, was also of his acquaintance and contributed an additional bronze edition of each of his portrait busts to this already remarkable private collection of Haskells. Stanley remembers;

"He had over thirty of them!"

Stanley shares his remarkable gregarity with frequent visitors, and readily enthralls them in the anecdotes of his early memories. He engages them with his refreshing familiarity with important figures in Art, Letters and Life from the early part of the last century. He also laughs at his memories as they return to him, and might ask you to read a poem that a war comrade, *Jim Guy*, wrote sixty years ago, as they idled some hours away. He served four years in The Royal Artillery.

"PRO RATRIA"
Sometime ago I came to know I'd got to join the army.
So with the rest, I took my test: The Lame; the Blind; the Barmy.
They tapped my chest beneath my vest, deplored my lack of gumption.
The job was done, I passed A1; I'd only got consumption.

The weeks passed on, my strength was gone.
The MO got quite nervous.
At last he said "you're not quite dead,
Grade 2 for active service"

At last I tired, my life expired, my soul, it went to serve.
My lifeless shell, condemned to hell.
To the staff of the 9th reserve. R.A.

To listen to his stories of the Great and the Good, as well as his companionable army friends is to come to know their names almost as contemporary personalities still enriching present cultural life and times. None of the remoteness and aridity that history can suffuse into generations past is there, as he reflects on his life, completely without sentiment, in his captivating and matter of fact way of telling.

He studied Painting at the Royal College of Art for 4 years in the 1920's when Sir William Rothenstein was Principal, and recalls a time when doing his Researches and Drawing in the British Museum Print Room, his absence from College caused Rothenstein some concern. Expecting severe upbraidings, Stanley was summoned to his Principal's Studio, and explanations sought. Rothenstein, a Society Painter, quizzed him closely, but was astonished, gratified and reassured when Stanley produced his full and detailed academically drawn portfolio to confirm his best endeavours. Thereafter, Stanley recalls, he was:

'left to get on with it'.

In 1930, he came second in the Rome scholarships for Mural Painting! Whilst in London and living with his aunt, Sally Taylor also a painter of considerable merit, and a spiritualist, at Radcliffe Gardens, Earls Court, Stanley spent one memorable afternoon in the company of Arthur Conan Doyle, who was there to buy paintings with his wife. He remembers the discussions on matters of the occult; and, (almost as an afterthought)... of the paintings he'd come to choose......

"He bought two, you know. Couldn't make his mind up".

On another occasion, as, he was about to enter the Royal College through its revolving doors, George Bernard Shaw, (who was being drawn by Rothenstein, in his series of red chalk studies of writers and artist), chose to make a speedy exit through the opposite side. Stanley explains how he almost lost his fingers as Shaw burst through, nearly trapping his hand in the rotating edge:

'He shot through, almost took me fingers off, never said sorry...
and roared off in his motor car in a cloud of smoke!!.

It wasn't long before commissions came his way. Alfred Kingsley Lawrence, Professor of Composition at the Royal College, engaged him as assistant in the production of the 'Bank of England Panels' in his fourth year, though initially Stanley had some doubts about taking the task on board;

"Lawrence had been in the trenches and had it rough.
He was prone to depression now and again.
He lived in his Studio, very plain and simple... He slept on the floor under a blanket,
and sometimes he would sleep on the overhead balcony in the studio.
Sometimes wouldn't move for two days..."

I admired Lawrence's paintings and drawings and his pastel drawings were brilliant. He was a Rome scholar with a great knowledge of Italian Painting and was a brilliant artist. He was also a member of the Royal Academy.

It was the first of many important Commissions to come his way. In World War Two as a soldier, he was transferred to the Fleet Air Arm in Yeovil for special duties. He was recognised for his abilities, and was asked as an unofficial War Artist, to produce the

Commemorative oil painting of the Bombing in Norway of the Tirpitz, which is now in the Fleet Airarm Museum, Yeovil, Somerset

"I had a model of the 'Tirpitz' sent down to me from London and
did my preliminary studies of it from the top of a ladder as the
Barracuda bombers would have seen it when they attacked. Anyway one day,
Commander Hollins brought Sir Arthur 'Bomber' Harris to see progress on the work.
I couldn't believe it was him, and he decided to sit on a stool close by,
and lifted his coat tails to sit down, but my palette and paints were on it!
I just managed to whip it away in time, or he'd have sat on the lot and got paint
all over his backside. Never mind the sinking of the Tirpitz....
I'd have been sunk if that had happened!!
And do you know, all the Top Brass on the camp were in such a
high state of alert because he was here; and all he wanted to do was sit
and talk to me about Spanish Painting; Murillo, Velázquez and his favourite, Goya.....
I remember thinking ... 'here is a man who sent hundreds of young airmen
to their deaths last night, and all he wants to talk about is Art and Painters'!!"
- perhaps it helped to relieve the awful strain he bore.

As his career progressed, from the 1930's, and into his post-war period, Stanley's academic prowess and dexterous painterly skills, began to focus his work as an artist of contemporary social realism. He also became a renowned teacher of painting starting his first Appointment as Painting Master at Newport School of Art. It was whilst he was there that he met a captivating eighteen year old student, Minnie Wright, who enchanted him completely. Shortly afterwards, they embarked on their lifetime romance, which came to cause some concern, particularly since Min was thirteen years younger:

"It was disapproved of, you know, but we tried to be sensible about it and
keep it a bit quiet; but the Principal got wind of it and called me in to lecture me.
I remember him shouting as I went into his office;
'LEWIS, IT'S ALL GOT TO STOP'.
Well, it was September 1939, and the War had just started,
so I thought about it and said;
'I see sir, well it's a bit late for that so I'd better invite you to my wedding'....!
Nothing more was said!!"

Stanley and Min were married for sixty four years. Throughout this time, they became a formidable team, totally engaged in a supportive, creative partnership of Painting, Drawing and Writing, and acutely aware that their respective abilities and opinions were eagerly sought and valued by peers of their own and later younger generations of Artists and Writers. Min was an imaginative and inventive skilled writer of journalistic reviews and fantasy prose, and much of her work included seventeen years of writing a weekly Children's story for the *'South Wales Evening News'* newspaper. Always well received, and with huge fond following of young readers. Stanley also produced the highly whimsical pen and ink drawings that accompanied them. Min's stories and the original drawings all still survive, and she continued to produce independent storybooks for children until she died.

As a Teacher and Painter, Stanley's stylistic versatility, accomplishment and pictorial content demonstrated not only a brilliant technical command of painting and draughtmanship, but also an acerbic and astute wit in his study of social detail. After the time spent teaching his subject at Newport, he was invited to the new Appointment of Principal of the Carmarthen School of Art, and with the reputation he took with him, built the college into a fine College of Art. He remained as Principal until he retired in 1968. He served 37 years in the teaching profession which included his 4 years with the army.

In 2002 a new audience would discover Stanley's work when, for the first time, an exhibition of his wartime paintings and drawings was shown at The Newport Museum and Art Gallery in South Wales. The following year aged 97 Stanley was invited to visit his hometown of Newport, which had recently been granted City Status. He was received by the Mayor of Newport and asked to sign his name beneath that of Her Majesty Queen Elizabeth ll and the Archbishop of Canterbury into the Civic Record at the Mansion House.

Altogether, this is a wonderful book with its pungent atmospheric reflection of bygone times, and an authentic reference to the quaint and peppery social arenas of the period. The work should not be underestimated in terms of the accuracy of its actual detail of daily life as Stanley and Min recorded it. Local personalities, absorbed in their eccentricities, and absurd hierarchies, are seen in the chaos and intimacy of their working lives. That was how it was, and how Dylan also saw it. This work has in fact now become *The* essential documentary reference that gives a complete corroboration to Dylan's own work, and must therefore be prized in some real academic measure as its closest confirmation.

Most of the detail in this Edition relates directly to 'Milkwood' and also catalogues Dylan's very *first production of the play*, with drawings and text; commentary and signed biographical references from the *actual First Players,* alongside drawings of the *Original Stage Settings*, produced as it was being performed (photography was impossible, it was too dark). All who have been involved in this revised First Edition, are sure that it will be well received, since it was always Min's special dream that it would be resurrected to be enjoyed once again, and Stanley's great hope in being able to dedicate it to his late wife, co-author and much loved lifelong companion.

Dr. Patrick Oates   Altrincham Cheshire 2003

PATRICK OATES
A Brief Professional Biography

Patrick Oates is an academically trained Figurative Fine Artist Sculptor and Ceramicist who exhibits work of a distinctly bold but detailed naturalistic style. His First Degree in Fine Art, specialising in Sculpture was undertaken in Birmingham in the 1960's studying under John Bridgeman A.R.C.A. His Masters Degree continued in Manchester with the late Keith Goodwin A.R.C.A; and subsequently his Doctorate in a Post-Medieval Classification of North Devon Slip Decorated Pottery.

After a career of over thirty years in Further and Higher Education, Patrick retired from the sector as the Head of a Northern English School of Art, to concentrate on commissioned works and promoting his interest in *Lifelong Learning* through the British *Adult Residential Colleges Association, (A.R.C.A.);* where he now delivers specialist Arts Programmes as an established visiting professor.

As a Historian, he is dedicated to the study of *20th century British Art Movements,* and the unique *eccentricities* of *Individual Contributors;* though he is also separately intrigued by the study of Ethnic and Ancient Civilisations. In these endeavours, he has travelled throughout the World, notably tours to India, Egypt, China, Mexico and North America. He plans to visit Peru and Chile and thereafter, Nigeria and West Africa. These Tours enable him to extensively photograph and record many sites of World Heritage, and this archive of material forms the basis of many of his specialist Arts lecture tours. He lives and works in Cheshire in the north west of England

Laugharne Corporation

The Portreeve
requests the pleasure of the company of

Mr. Stanley Lewis.

to Breakfast at the Memorial Hall, on
Sunday, October 7th, 1962, at 9 a.m.
and to Divine Service at St. Martin's
Church at 11 a.m.

SUNNY HILL,
LAUGHARNE.   R.S.V.P.

WESTERN MAIL, TUESDAY, SEPTEMBER 25, 1962

LETTERS TO THE EDITOR

Why Did Dylan stay in Laugharne?

SIR - Perhaps Islwyn Williams bought a bunch of sour grapes in Laugharne that brought on the belly ache?

The TWW programme, "Wales and the West," depicting Laugharne in all its glory was the best I have seen, and may have been even better had the poet Betjeman with his quiet cultured voice been the commentator.

So Dylan hated Laugharne, hated the quiet dignity and beauty of the little town that inspired him to write his best works, hated Sir John's Hill and Fern Hill and the everlapping waves of the River Taf that flowed past his door?

For the same cost Dylan could have lived and starved at Llantwit Major, Swansea, Cardiff, or anywhere else in Wales; he was not tied by the responsibilities of a job and, being a married man with a family, was old enough to choose his company, his pub and his place of abode, yet he chose Laugharne because it had and still has everything a poet requires.

In all Dylan's writings I have not yet found loathing or hatred for the little town he adopted to live in, for it gave him too much to be despised.

As for the indifference of the Laugharne people towards Wales's greatest poet, is a prophet ever appreciated in his home town?

MIN LEWIS
Laugharne.

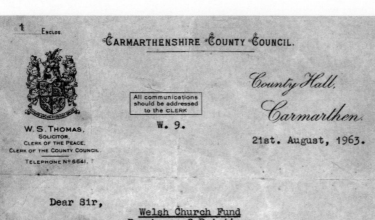

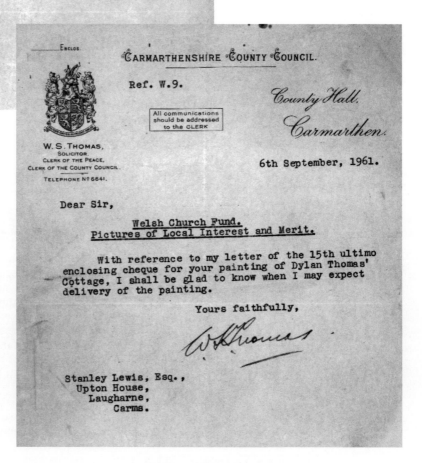

"Old Cockle Factory, Laugharne" and "Dylan Thomas' Cottage",
Oil Paintings by Stanley Lewis, Sold to Carmarthenshire County Council

Derek Gardner 13d Sheffield Terrace Kensington Church Street London W8 Park 3210

DG/jam   September 27th, 1963.

Dear Min,

            Thank you for your two letters.

            I have had the Dobson people round for
drinks and given them my own enthusiastic
account of Laugharne.

            They have borne the MS away with them
and this morning I had a 'phone call to say
that it certainly had the makings of a book.
What would we need in terms of payment, etc.

            I said I thought you would be "fairly
modest in your requirements," as I know that
you want to see the book published; as long
as you get a good royalty rate and a good
proportion of U. S. sales that is what matter

            I have told them that Stanley will do
the illustrations rather more quickly than
I CHALLENGE THE DARK SEA, so things look a
little more hopeful than with previous
publishers.

                        Yours,

                        Derek

Mrs. Min Lewis,
Upton House,
Laugharne,
CARMS.

Derek Gardner 13d Sheffield Terrace Kensington Church Street London W8 Park 3210

DG/jam   May 12th, 1964.

Dear Min.,

            At long last your patience has been rewarded, and I am
delighted to report that Dobson will publish the book.

            It has taken a good deal of persuasion but I am sure they
will do you well.   The important thing now is that we must have
some illustrations and until these are ready, of course, production
of the book cannot be started. I had been hoping that Stanley would
send one or two specimens but I am sure you will now be able to
encourage him.

            The Dobsons say that while they very much liked the illustrat-
ions for I CHALLENGE THE DARK SEA they think that the ones for this
book should be less formal and more relaxed. I believe we have
already discussed this and I am certain Stanley knows what is
required.   The Dobsons envisage about twenty illustrations and say
that these should not be confined to Laugharne alone but should
include the surrounding countryside and possibly a drawing or two
of Swansea.

            We have tentatively discussed an advance of £100, but they
will not pay this until they have the illustrations. I imagine that
Stanley will be able to prepare these during the summer holidays,
so, if the book is to be issued next summer, they should be in the
publishers' office by the middle of September - the average
gestation period for a book being similar to that for humans.

            I will go ahead and have a contract drawn up so that you can
sign and have witnessed by a local dignitary while we are in
Laugharne next week.

            I am writing you separately about beds and other things, but
thought that this one should be typed for the files.

                        Yours,

                        wt. Derek g.

                        Dictated by Mr. Gardner and signed on
                              his behalf.

Mrs. Min Lewis,
Upton House,
Laugharne,
CARMS.

Two letters from Min Lewis's Literary Agent.

THE NEW ILLUSTRATED
LAUGHARNE
AND
DYLAN THOMAS

by
MIN LEWIS

illustrated by
STANLEY LEWIS

Stanley Lewis.

SADDLEWORTH
TAYLOR & CLIFTON

*For permission to quote copyright material the author
and publishers thank*
(John M. Brinnin Dylan Thomas in America) *and Messrs
David Higham Associates Ltd*
(Dylan Thomas Under Milk Wood, Quite Early One Morning, Portrait of the
Artist as a Young Dog, Collected Poems)
& (John M. Brinnin Dylan Thomas in America)

*We would also like to thank the following for permission
to quote from their magazines/publications:*
Country Quest Magazine
Western Mail
South Wales Evening Post
Carmarthen Journal
The Mid Wales Journal
South Wales Argus
Carmarthenshire County Council
Newport Museum & Art Gallery
*Some writings and publications have been impossible to trace despite our very best efforts.
We thank them here for their works and inspiration.*

The British Library Cataloguing-in-Publication Data.
A catalogue record for this book is available from British Library
ISBN 0-9547572-0-3
Contact us by email bev@bjlelec.co.uk
Fax 01457 833700

First published in Great Britain in 1967 by
Dobson Books Ltd, 80 Kensington Church Street, London W8
Film set by Yendall & Co Ltd, London
Printed By Latimer Trend & Co Ltd, Whitstable
Bound by Webb Son & Co Ltd, London and Ferndale
Revised first edition 2004
Printed by Taylor & Clifton Ltd.
130 High Street, Uppermill, Saddleworth OL3 6BT
Published by Jennifer Heywood

CONTENTS

I am much indebted for information concerning Dylan Thomas
to my many friends in and around Laugharne.

A FORMER Newport woman is to have a book published on Laugharne in relation to **Dylan Thomas** - "Laugharne and the Poet" - and the book is to be illustrated by her husband, a former art master at Newport Art College.

Mrs. Min Lewis, now living at Upton House, Laugharne, where the poet spent much of his life, is a short story writer and has had many children's stories published, as well as magazine articles. This is her first book to be accepted for publication, however.

Mrs. Lewis was born at Little Oak, Rogerstone, and went to Arlington House School at Stow Hill. Later, she attended Drayton High School, which was eventually demolished to make room for the Civic Centre.

Later, she became a student at the art college, where her husband, **Mr. Stanley Lewis,** was teaching.

Mr. Lewis painted "The Welsh Mole Catcher," the star picture of the Royal Academy in 1937, which was later bought by Newport Art Gallery.

After the war, Mr. Lewis became principal of Carmarthen School of Art and the couple moved to Carmarthenshire, where they have lived ever since.

Above, Mrs. Lewis is seen with the recorder of Laugharne, Alderman Fleming Williams, who witnessed the signing of the contract for the new book in the presence of Mrs. Lewis' literary agent, Mr. Derek Gardner.

SOUTH WALES ARGUS May 25, 1964

Launching of Min's Laugharne & Dylan Thomas in Brown's Hotel, 1967

Signing Publisher's Contract of Laugharne & Dylan Thomas in Glan-y-mor Grounds, 1964

Country Quest

THE MAGAZINE OF WALES AND THE BORDER · Published March, June, September, December.

CAXTON PRESS - OSWESTRY

TELEPHONE 3374

GG/ED/CQ   4th February, 1966

Mrs. Min Lewis,
Water Meadows,
St. Clears,
Carms.

Dear Mrs. Lewis,

    I'm glad to hear the good news about the publication of your book.

    What I would have liked is an article dealing fairly comprehensively with Dylan's sources - that is the real people on whom he formed his characters.Mr. Watts, the basis for Mog Edwards is a good example.

    The enclosed is not quite the kind of thing I had in mind.

                        Yours sincerely,

                        Glyn Griffiths.

The original Country Quest letter -1966 which refers to the article overleaf when Min Lewis subsequently wrote 'When Dylan Met Captain Cat' and 'Mr Mog in a Boater' published in Country Quest Magazine in 1966.

DYLAN THOMAS was not particular about the way he dressed. When living in Laugharne he was a familiar sight walking the cliffs in untidy baggy trousers, his coat pockets weighed down with a bottle of beer, and a jar of pickled onions.

On the other hand he was most anxious that his son, Llewellyn, should not be ridiculed at school for looking odd. He was angry once with Caitlin when she darned the boy's grey school socks with red wool.

It was fatherly Dylan who wrote to Mr. William Watts, draper of Gwalia House, Laugharne, with instructions that Llewellyn should be fitted with wellington boots, for he wrote: Dear Mr Watts, Will you please see that Llewellyn buys a pair of wellington boots that fit him properly? I will be up later to settle with you. Thank you, Yours sincerely, Dylan Thomas".

The one and only draper's shop in the main street of Laugharne catered not only for the comfort of the body, but for the satisfaction of the feet as well.

Gwalia House stands opposite the whitewashed tower of the Town Hall, with the striking but

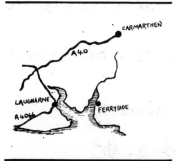

unpredictable clock. Inside, wellington boots hung from the ceiling, like sides of bacon. Mr. William Watts, who was affectionately known as Billo, has been dead some years, but his daughter, Mrs. Gwen Jones, is convinced that Dylan had her father's mode of dress in mind when he created Mr. Mog Edwards, the draper of Cloth Hall, in his play for

Mr. Mog in a boater

by

MIN LEWIS

Did Dylan Thomas have William Watts in mind when he created Mr Mog Edwards, the draper of Cloth Hall in Under Milk Wood?

voices, 'Under Milk Wood'.

"Dada always wore a straw hat, a butterfly collar and a bow die. He was very particular about his dress", Mrs. Jones told me, and to prove it she gave me a photograph of Mr. Watts sitting on the shore. But that is where the similarity ends, for Mr. Watts was a much respected married man, quite unlike Mr. Mog Edwards, who told the world that he was "a draper mad with love".

To the north of the main street, almost opposite the lychgate of the church, is Horsepool Road, a narrow, attractive street leading down to a stone bridge over a stream. In a tiny cottage in Horsepool road, once lived Rosie Probert.

Many years ago, a little girl spending a holiday with Rosie Probert, was fascinated by the ducks that swam up and down stream. Eager to see the ducks, she ran excitedly to the bridge, but leaning too far over the parapet, lost her balance, fell into the stream and was drowned.

Although Dylan never knew Rosie Probert, he heard the story and obviously used her name as a character in 'Under Milk Wood'.

The late Alderman E. V. Williams who for many years was organist at Laugharne Church, was asked by curious visitors whether he was Organ Morgan, and like most Laugharne people, he was not annoyed but merely amused by these questions. He was able to get his own back when they asked him to show them the memorial to Dylan Thomas. For standing in the aisle of the church he pointed to a stained glass window and said: "That window was erected in memory of Sir Guy de Brian, who granted the charter to the Burgesses of Laugharne in 1307".

Then looking very serious, he pointed to the opposite window, and, with his tongue in his cheek, said: "That window was erected in memory of Polly Garter!". Amazingly the strangers, unaware that he was joking, simply gasped: "Was it really?"

When 'Under Milk Wood' was first performed in London, many of Dylan's Laugharne friends were invited, and after the performance, Alderman Billy Williams was asked: "Well, Billy, how did you like it?"

"Good God" exclaimed Billy', "I thought I was back in Laugharne".

Min's article in Country Quest magazine in 1966

'THERE is no nation yet known in either hemisphere where the people of all conditions are more in want of some cordial to keep up their spirits than in this of ours'. This statement by Jonathan Swift could well have been uttered by Dylan Thomas who frequently visited the eight public houses in Laugharne.

This mysterious township where life changes slowly and where they keep up the customs of another age with such conviction and pride, has through the years lost many of its pubs but hangs on to its ancient undated and unsealed charter.

Almost opposite the lych gate of St. Martin's Church is the Farmers Arms where the landlady affectionately known as Miss Annie writes the debts in chalk on beer barrels. When the barrels are empty the debts are taken away but are never forgotten. Near the vicarage where lime trees slow down the traffic stands the pub called The Green Dragon, a friendly pub with a wolf whistling parrot. Along King Street where the cherry trees bloom in Spring, and where in Autumn the leaves fall and clog the gutters, stands the well-known Browns Hotel, and on the corner of the street once known as Hangman Street (because the scaffold was at the east end of it) but renamed Victoria Street in 1838 in honour of Queen Victoria's coronation, is the pub called The Mariners.

Down the steep road called Wogan Street is the Grist Square marked with a stone cross in the middle of the road. During the 19th century, funeral processions marched three times around the cross; this custom is revived every three years on Whit Monday when the common walk takes place and the procession of walkers march around the cross three times before proceeding to more strenuous ground.

There are three public houses on the Grist — The Fountain Inn, The Corporation Arms, (the recorder of Laugharne was the landlord when Dylan drank there), and the Cross House. On the road to Pendine is the last Laugharne pub called The Carpenters Arms.

There lived in Laugharne a seafaring man called John Thomas, Holloway. He lived in a tiny house under a bank, called Myrtle Cottage which is near Holloway fields; he was master of his own ship called the *Naughtless* that sailed to Bidecombe in Devon for bricks and to Kidwelly in Carmarthenshire for coal.

Where Dylan met Captain Cat

BY

MIN LEWIS

whose book on Laugharne is due to be published this Summer

Johnny Thomas was a regular drinker at the Cross House where he met and yarned to Dylan Thomas. Johnny Thomas was boastful of his sea-faring days, which he relived in imagination when he became too old to handle a ship. He lived to the ripe age of eighty nine to become the oldest shareholder in Laugharne. Towards the end of his life he became blind but was able with the assistance of a strong walking stick and a loud voice to find his way to the Cross House for his daily pints of beer.

On his death bed he pleaded for some cool clear water from the Lakes and some good strong beer. Many Laugharne people are convinced that Dylan's Captain Cat, so vividly portrayed in *Under Milk Wood*, was inspired by Johnny Thomas, Holloway. The *Naughtless* had a tragic end; it sank off the Mumbles.

Dylan did not become a burgess of Laugharne, probably because it would have cost him three guineas plus a tip for the jury, and Dylan did not have that kind of money to spare. Had he been a son of a burgess it would have cost him one guinea plus a tip for the jury, but he would never have become a shareholder, for it usually takes from twenty to twenty five years to become one of these, and to claim a share it is essential to live in Laugharne up to midnight for six months.

Richard Bevan was Portreeve of Laugharne when Samuel Pepys became a burgess of Portsmouth in 1662. Pepys recorded the event in his diary:— 'This afternoon after dinner comes Mr Stephenson, one of the burgesses of the Town, to tell me that the Mayor and the burgesses did desire my acceptance of a burgessship and were ready at the Mayors to make me one. So I went and there they were all ready, and did with much civility give me my oath and after the oath, did by custom shake me all by the hand, so I took them to a tavern and made them drink, and paying the reckoning went away'.

The Portreeve's breakfast takes place on a Sunday immediately following Big Court night when the Portreeve is elected or re-elected and takes the oath of loyalty to Church and state.

The portreeve provides the breakfast which is attended by more than a hundred male guests. Women are allowed only to prepare and serve the food which consists of cold cooked meats, bread and butter, tea or coffee and cigarettes. No intoxicating liquor is allowed to be drunk in the Memorial Hall where the breakfast is usually held. The breakfast is followed by a Church service and afterwards much liquor is consumed and there are many aching heads the following day.

Chancellor Sydney B. Williams was the vicar and Portreeve of Laugharne when Dylan was a guest in 1937-1938. After all the speeches were made by the honoured guests, Dylan proposed the vote of thanks to the ladies.

Perhaps one day Laugharne, so proud of its charter, customs, church, cockles and curlews will feel honoured that Dylan Thomas who was not born at Laugharne chose to live there for fifteen years, and rests forever in the churchyard where owls live in the yews, and where death hath no dominion.

Min's article in Country Quest magazine in 1966

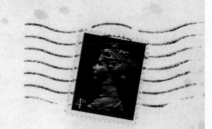

Miss Min Lewis,
   c/o Brown's Hotel,
   LLACHARN,
   Laugharne,
   Sir Gaerfyrddin.

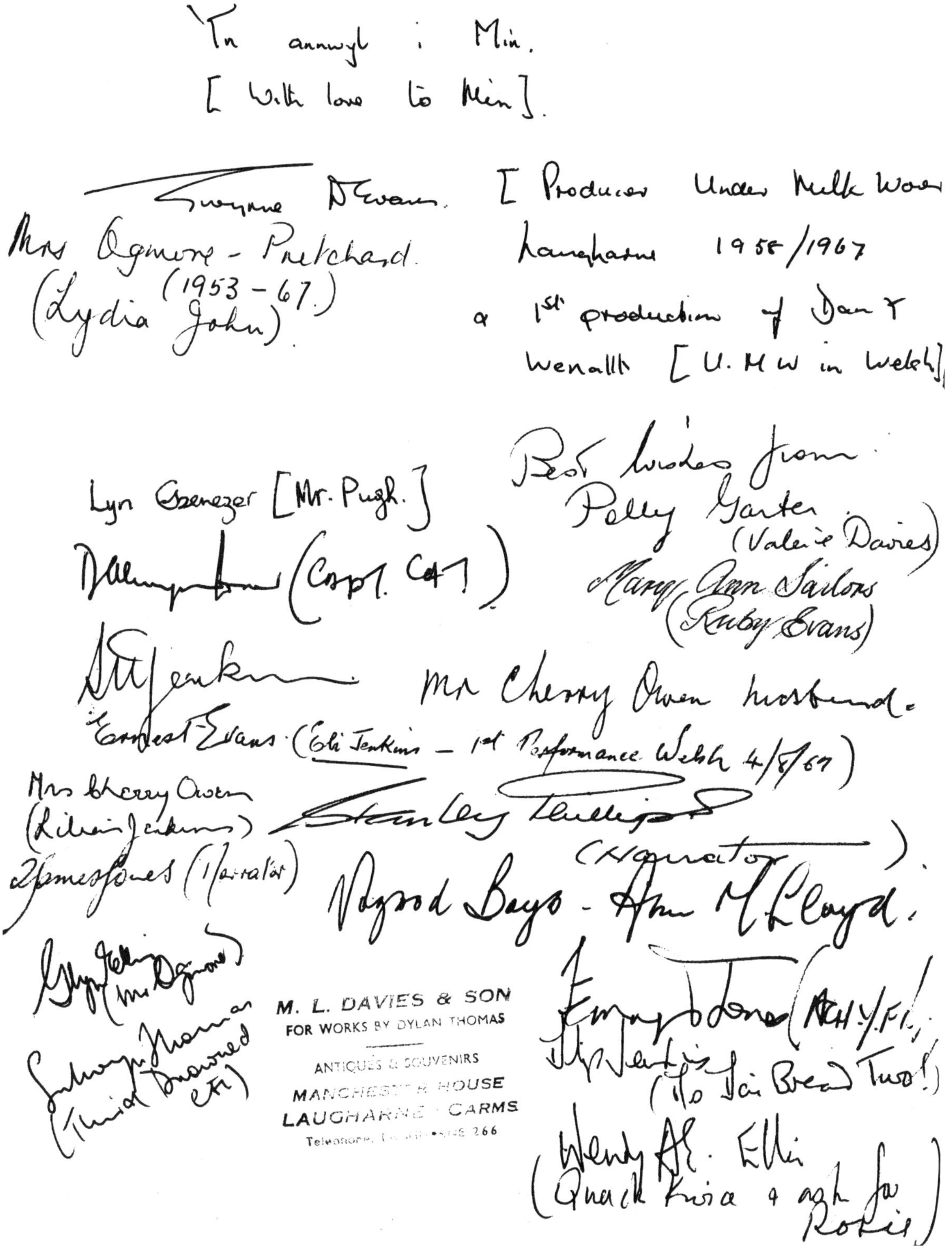

Yn annwyl : Min.
[With love to Min].

Gwynne D'Evans. [Producer Under Milk Wood
Mrs Ogmore - Pritchard. Laugharne 1958/1967
(Lydia John) (1953 - 67.) a 1st production of Dan y
Wenallt [U. M W in Welsh]

Lyn Ebenezer [Mr. Pugh.]   Best wishes from
                                   Polly Garter
          (Capt. Cat)   (Valerie Davies)
                                   Mary Ann Sailors
                                    (Ruby Evans)

          Jenkins   Mr Cherry Owen husband.
Ernest Evans (Eli Jenkins – 1st Performance Welsh 4/8/67)
Mrs Cherry Owen
(Lilian Jenkins)   Stanley Phillips
James Jones (Narrator)   (Narrator   )
              Rosrod Bays - Ann M Lloyd.

         Emyr Jones (No. 1, F.,
          (No Jai Bread Two!)
       Wendy A. Ellin
       (Quack Frisa & ask for
                         Rosie)

Signatures of Llaregyb Players

Dylan Thomas's grave in St. Martin's Church, Laugharne

It was November dreary and damp cold in the small township. Across the desolate bay, curlews and seagulls cried, a haunting tribute as the water flowed, filling in the cracks and crannies, listening to the Dolls and Dannies as they stood and gossiped, prayed and prepared for a poet's funeral.

They brought Dylan back to Laugharne from far-a-way America where he had completed *Under Milk Wood,* back to rest awhile at the Pelican, a tall house in King Street where Dylan's mother rented a flat.

Laugharne was grey with mist and mystery, there were strangers everywhere, tall and short, thin and fat, no one knew where they came from, they might have come down from the clouds with the rain, it seemed more like the yearly carnival than the funeral of a Welsh poet.

Mourners filled the town's seven pubs, drinking beer and spirits while they waited; what else was there to do in Laugharne? The main bell of St Martin's Church at the north end, tolled mournfully its low slow funeral boom, echoing across the desolate countryside, proclaiming death like an Old Testament prophet, as Will John landlord of the Fountain Inn and sexton pulled the solitary bell-rope.

Men and women, young and old peeped curiously from behind coloured curtains and pub windows watching the long slow procession of mourners following the cortège, wondering and remarking on the size of his funeral.

Only people, respected and respectable like ministers and councillors, deacons and chapel-regulars had big funerals. If Dylan Thomas was respected, they knew not why.

The six bearers of Laugharne who carried the coffin from the lych-gate to the church were friends and confederates of the poet. Phil Richards, landlord of the Cross Inn, Douglas Williams, son of Ebbie and Ivy Williams of Brown's Hotel, Billy Williams, District Councillor, Howard Dark, Dai Thomas and Billy Thomas.

They carried him into the ancient porch where a grey stone set into the wall faced them with the stark truth of life and death.

> Behould the place wher I do ly,
> As you are now so once was I,
> As I am now so shalt thou be,
> Cut of by death and follow me. (1690)

Chancellor Williams, Vicar of Laugharne, conducted the service and Dylan, who once wrote, 'I've been living now for fifteen years, or centuries, in this timeless, beautiful, barmy (both spellings) town,' was buried in the new churchyard over the concrete bridge. There, among marble monuments in memory of lesser people a white wooden cross now marks his resting place with the simple words painted in black:

> In Memory of Dylan Thomas
> Died Nov. 9th 1953. R.I.P.

The ceremony over, the mumbling black-garbed mourners left the church to congregate in the pubs, to discuss the virtues of the deceased since vices are forgotten on the funeral day.

'He should 'ave stayed 'ere,' they said. 'He wouldn't be lying lonely up there if he'd stayed in Laugharne.'

'He only drank beer in Laugharne, good beer from the barrel, I never saw him sample whisky in my life!"

'I want everybody to be drunk at my funeral,' Dylan once declared in a cool Laugharne pub. 'Let there be no mournful faces, just bury me in the Green Banks.'

'He was a good sort,' a drinker declared. 'He never caused no trouble in Laugharne, he liked a game of nap and a game of darts, he wasn't a bad throw either.'

For fifteen barmy years, Dylan Thomas lived beside the sea and the green hills, beneath the wood damp with dripping trees, in a township which has survived the centuries, to emerge victorious, for he is now as much a part of the history of Laugharne as the castle ruin and the church, the medieval customs and the charter.

The damp dreary autumn day faded as meekly as it began, and soon a sea mist hid the green fields of Llanstephan and the red-gorsed glory of Sir John's Hill. Lights were lit and curtains drawn, not in respect for the dead but for the night, hiding the Welsh dressers adorned with lustre jugs and willow-patterned plates, keeping the frost from the pot ferns, busy-lizzies and geraniums, while the wind moaned amongst the tangled branches of the twisted yews, and in the ancient churchyard owls called to one another.

Ruins of Laugharne Castle

King Street, Laugharne

Sketch of The Boat House, Laugharne

The TOWNSHIP of Laugharne where Dylan Thomas lived, drank, and wrote much of his work is as different from Swansea, where he was born, as chalk is from cheese.

Laugharne once named Abercorran and then Talycharn, derived its name from its situation at the mouth of the River Corran. It is a small township, no bigger than an ordinary Welsh village, steeped in history and tradition and proud of it. It is the last example of a medieval corporation still retaining its customs, it is a writer's dream and a painter's heaven.

They do not speak highly of Laugharne in neighbouring villages. Laugharne is said to be the place where they fight with glass bottles. 'Larnies are rough,' people claim, 'and they run up and down the football pitch with umbrellas scaring the opponents.'

Perhaps the neighbours envy Laugharne its independant air, its unique privilege of being a township, its portreeve, recorder and burgesses, its cockles and curlews, the sweet-scented wallflowers growing from sandstone rock, the hedges of blackthorne white in spring, the smell of seaweed, cherry blossom, the clock that always points to opening time at closing time, owls in the churchyard, bats in the belfry and jackdaws in the chimneys.

Laugharne marks the Eastern boundary of the part of South West Wales known as 'Little England beyond Wales', Welsh is rarely understood or spoken there, for they have a characteristic dialect of their own, thou and thee being commonly used. Indeed Laugharne possesses few strictly Welsh characteristics, probably because the Flemings settled there in the twelfth century.

William of Malmesbury who lived at the time of this settlement wrote:

The Welsh perpetually rebelling, were subjugated by King Henry I, who discovered a mode of counteracting their designs by stationing in their county Flemings to be a barrier to them.

The old poet Drayton, in his Fifth Song refers to the floods in Flanders which originally drove the Flemings to Britain:

They also settled along the coast of County Carmarthen, their presence is very apparent in Laugharne where are many tucking mills introduced by them.

The immigrants did not acquire the language of the people among whom they settled, nor did they retain their own. Instead, they spoke good pure English, and no one is able to account for this. Indeed Giraldus Cambrensis thought the whole district of Pembrokeshire so anglicised that he called it Anglia Transwalliana or England beyond Wales.

During the nineteenth century, Laugharne was colonised by the English. 'For some years,' wrote a contemporary writer, 'it has been the resort of English families of good position in society, who seek retirement and a spot where the necessaries of life are purchased at a reasonable price.'

But Laugharne's history did not begin with the Flemings. The castle was first attributed to Rhys ap Gruffuff the last of the Princes of South Wales who was forced to acknowledge King Henry of England as his overlord. He paid homage to Henry II when the King visited Laugharne after returning from Ireland in 1172, and the main Laugharne street is said to have been named King Street to commemorate this royal visit. Later the castle passed into the hands of Sir Gwydo de Brione who granted the Charter of Laugharne to the burgesses in the reign of Edward I.

A descendant of Sir Gwydo was the celebrated Sir Guy de Brian, K.G., Lord High Admiral of Edward III and Richard II. The north-east window in the nave bears the de Brian coat of arms and also contains a portrait of Edward III.

Centuries later, King Henry VIII gave the castle to his natural son Sir John Perrott who converted it into a mansion. Through succeeding centuries the castle experienced many changes, but with age and neglect it became a ruin. Now it wears its drapes of green ivy graciously and in a mysterious haunting way still commands admiration.

The privileges and customs of Laugharne have proved more enduring than its castle, for every two weeks the Grand Jury, consisting of twenty-one men, sit to conduct business in the Town Hall. Antlers hang from the courtroom walls, there are unpadded benches to sit on, and a Victorian cast-iron grate for heating.

The Town Hall which is situated next to the castle, has a white-washed square tower with a clock; the clock roof is topped by a golden weathercock as fickle as the weather.

The head of the corporation is the portreeve, an office instituted by the charter. A portreeve does not mean the reeve of a seaport as so often misinterpreted, but the reeve of a walled or market town. The salary of the portreeve who is elected by the burgesses is twenty pounds a year.

Big Court night is held on a Monday evening in October when the portreeve takes the oath of loyalty to church and state. After the meeting he is chaired and carried to various local pubs where he buys beer for men and women and lemonade for the children.

On Sunday morning following Big Court night, the portreeve provides a breakfast consisting of cold cooked meat, bread and butter, tea or coffee and cigarettes for more than a hundred male guests. Speeches are made by the chief guests and, according to the medieval custom, the women who serve and wait are seen but not heard. After the breakfast, the guests walk in slow procession to St Martin's Church for morning service, later they celebrate in true Laugharne fashion.

In past centuries, the portreeve was a man of substance with power to deal with local criminal cases. It is recorded in John Donn's Hundred Court:

1. There is no outlaw in this town.

2. There has not been anyone convicted for felony or murder for the last eighteen years.

3. There ought to be a pillory and a trip cart [used as a ducking stool] and the Common Attorneys have been ordered to provide them by the next Court.

That was in the sixteenth century; four centuries later, during Dylan's stay at Laugharne, a murder was committed in a tiny four-roomed cottage in Clifton Street. The victim, a poor lonely old spinster called Lizzie Thomas worked hard to earn a few shillings, she regularly cleaned the church and washed the choir surplices, not in a modern washing machine, but in a wooden tub, she ironed them with a flat iron heated on the fire. Sometimes she returned the laundered surplices to the church at night, which

14

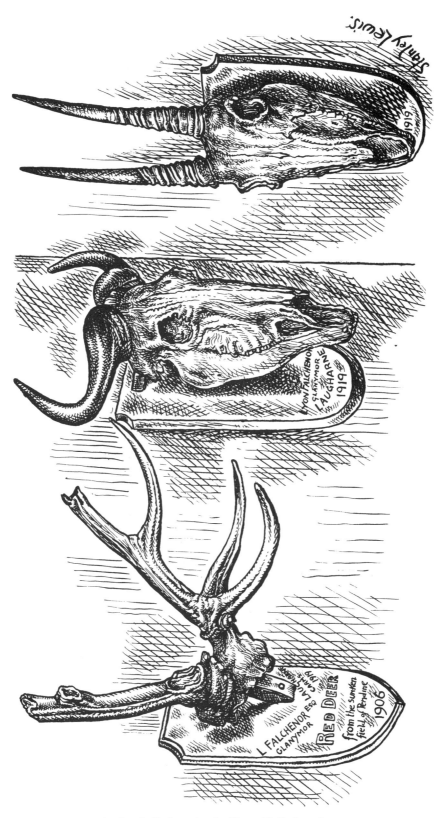

Antler skulls hanging in Town Hall, Laugharne

Sketch of stage set of Under Milk Wood, Laugharne, 1958

Mr and Mrs Pugh

Captain Cat

caused her neighbour to remark, 'One night you'll get hit on the head going up that dark lane.' But Lizzie bravely replied, 'Who would want to murder an old woman like me?' Who indeed?

Weeks before the murder was committed, Lizzie had an idea that someone had been in her cottage while she was out, probably searching for her hard earned money which she kept hidden under the mattress, but Larnies are trusting people.

About six o'clock on a damp misty Saturday on January 10th, 1953, Lizzie Thomas was hit on the head with a blunt instrument and died without regaining consciousness. A short time before she died, she had called opposite at Fred Phillip's small grocery shop for sweets, at six o'clock the shop door was still open but Fred heard nothing. Next door to the grocery shop, the Edmunds of East Hill farm were milking the cows, they heard a sharp shrill cry but thinking a dog had been hit by a passing car paid no further attention to it.

A short while afterwards, Dylan's next door neighbour, a deaf mute called Budha, who lived alone at the Ferry House after the death of his uncles, and was no Asiatic God but a simple man forced to. live within himself because of his afflictions, was suspected and arrested.

It was difficult to accuse or condemn a man unable to defend himself, for he had no knowledge of the deaf and dumb language, although by signs he was able to make the locals understand his wants in the pubs.

Budha was eventually acquitted and is now being looked after in a Carmarthen home. The murder remains unsolved, although the obvious motive was money. The murderer did not gain by the crime, because the money was found intact, but the locals mourned a poor old lady whose tragic end brought fear and suspicion to Laugharne.

'It wasn't safe to talk to your neighbour, maid,' a local man told me. 'Everyone was under suspicion, it was like the bloody gestapo!'

During the Civil War and the period leading to the restoration of Charles II in 1660, the portreeves were in full charge of Laugharne affairs and seemed not unduly worried by the political situation.

In 1646, the portreeve gave money to the poor at Christmas, Easter and Whit Sunday, paid for a new lock and chain for the jail, paid three shillings and sixpence for a shroud for Mary Price. Other duties included paying £1.4.0 to Colonel Butlar of Carmarthen for the town's protection.

In 1650, Portreeve Thomas Bevan paid money to distressed Irishmen fleeing from their native country. Four shillings and sixpence was spent on drink for the Common Walk.

In 1653, Portreeve William Gilbert paid sixpence for a grave for a stranger who died in August, and fourpence for a man to wash him. Some years later, Alice Price had to sweep the streets towards the church five times to earn a shilling.

On the restoration of Charles II, Portreeve John Perrot paid £2. 16. 0 to Sir Sackville Crowe the Lord of the Manor, for an ox to roast at the celebrations, and for the Common Walk he paid for one barrel of beer and tobacco.

The Common Walk takes place every three years on Whit-Monday morning, with the performance of beating the bounds.

*　　　*　　　*　　　*

I was on the Common Walk of 1963.

It was chilly at 5.30 in the morning, but the first rays of sun penetrating the blue haze heralded the prospects of a warm day.

Laugharne was bustling with people some to take part in, others to give a send off to the Common Walk, and of course to sample the refreshments freely given in the Town Hall, people sipped steaming coffee or tea and ate buttered currant buns. As I fought my way into the overcrowded courtroom for a cup of coffee, a recent resident of Laugharne asked me, 'What is it about Laugharne that is so different from other places? Its ancient customs cannot make all that difference. Somehow I feel it's got a cosmopolitan air.'

Looking around at the many eager happy faces, I wondered too, for Laugharne is as damp and cold as other Welsh towns and villages, its houses often shrouded in mournful grey mists, yet on important occasions Laugharne comes to life with gusto, for both young and old have few inhibitions as they enjoy their way of life. Out in the street cameras clicked, and it was rumoured that a man from television was filming part of the walk.

'I hope he doesn't take me,' said one bashful onlooker, 'I've come out in my rags today.'

She need not have worried, for everyone wore rags, old pullovers that had not seen the light of day for years, wellington boots, and trousers baggy and patched were the proper wear for a twenty-one-mile walk up hill and down dale, following the well-worn corporation banner that fluttered in the breeze.

Three times we marched around the Town Hall and then down to the Grist where we marched three times around the Cross. The Cross was a parting of the ways where young children and elderly people bade us good beating, for only the toughest could survive the strenuous walk over such rough ground. The route led to the Strand and to the ascent of Sir John's Hill. There the leaders stopped to ask a woman to name the spot. 'Gorse Bank,' she said hopefully. 'Wrong,' everyone shouted with laughter, and the leaders turned her upside down to smack her bottom.

Breathlessly we marched on, climbing over thorn hedges, ducking under barbed wire, walking across dew drenched fields where cows stood in curious groups watching us before coming to greet us. Every inch of the way must be trodden if the burgesses were to claim the parcels of land which they lease to local farmers.

Walking across unfamiliar land, and seeing Laugharne awakening in the early morning was a refreshing sight. We came to places with fascinating names, Skerry and Fern Hill which we climbed. Perched on the hillside it looked majestic in its green glory with trees of white and pink may shimmering in the sunlight, and banks of pink campion and bluebells scenting the air.

We scrambled up and down hill, through farmyards, past white-washed barns, across patches of slimy cow-dung and mud, warily avoiding badger sets and foxholes. Down Gypsy Lane and Dead Man's Lane. As time passed it grew hotter and hotter until young men and girls discarded sweaters and tied them around their waists. We marched on, for hunger pains tormented us, but we were happy in the knowledge that breakfast was awaiting us at Halfpenny Furze.

Before breakfast we tackled Featherbed Lane, and truthfully it was no feather bed; for the lane which was shaded by high hedges was wet with water from fresh earth springs, and three steps forward meant two receding ones.

At Halfpenny Furze, the helpers were awaiting us with Portreeve Douglas Bradshaw.

18

Laugharne

After the Portreeve's Breakfast marching to St. Martin's Church, Laugharne

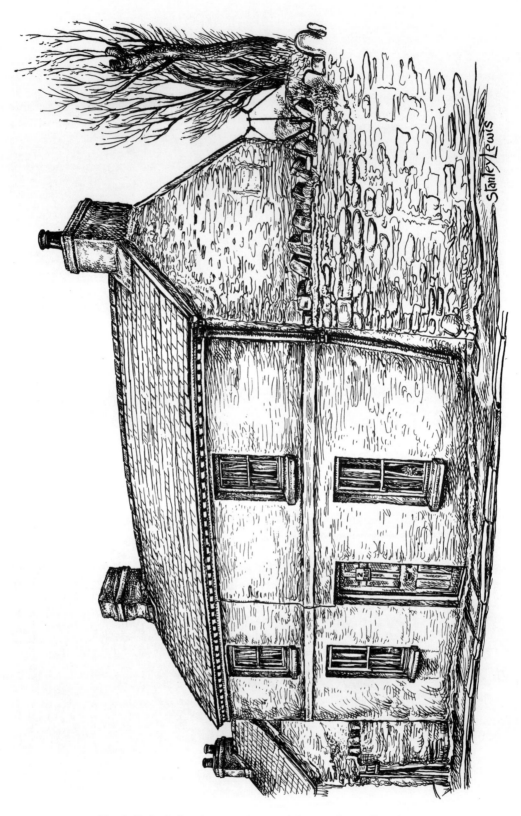

'Eros' - Dylan's first home at the top of Gosport Street, Laugharne

wearing the ceremonial chain of gold cockleshells. There was tea and beer and bottles of lemonade to drink, and bread-baskets full of sandwiches to eat. Never did breakfast taste so good, for never were appetites so ravenous.

Soon it was time to proceed with the walk, but here I bade them farewell, leaving them in happy spirits as they marched on singing like a happy band of warriors. Later I joined them at Cross Inn on the Laugharne road for lunch. Visitors passing by in cars, gazed in surprise at the vast picnic party of sweating walkers.

The Common Walk was coming to an end for another three years, and the Burgesses of Laugharne had again claimed the right to retain their land.

$$* \qquad * \qquad * \qquad *$$

Some time ago the lower portion of Laugharne called the Grist was the poorest and roughest part. There, fighting was a part of everyday life and a common expression arose which is still sometimes jokingly used, 'Up street with the toffs, and down street with the toughs.'

Dylan's first Laugharne home was a small cottage at the top of Gosport Street now called Eros. Like most Laugharne cottages at that time it was primitive having no sanitation or modern amenities. The front faced the main road, the back had a splendid view of the bay and the marsh, and this was the nearest house to Sir John's Hill that Dylan lived in.

> Over Sir John's Hill
> The Hawk on fire hangs still.

Sir John's Hill derives its name from Sir John Perrott, owner of the castle, who wished to build a house on top of the hill as a lookout for pirates infesting the coast at that time. An outer wall was erected but the house was not built.

The hill, a gradual incline starting from the Strand, winds aimlessly between tall trees and dangerous drops until it reaches a point rewarded by a fine view of Carmarthen Bay and most of the Bristol Channel to Lundy and Hartland Point in Devonshire.

To the right of the hill lies the low marshland called the Burrows and Laugharne sands. There amongst the sand dunes nestle small farms called The Gin Shop, Salt Marsh, Malt House, Longridge, Causeway and others, and Coygen quarry, where the celebrated Coygen Cave was discovered. In this cave, traces of life more than 50,000 years ago have been found by a team of students led by Dr Charles McBurney, lecturer in prehistoric archaeology at Cambridge University, who established that it had been inhabited by a Neanderthal tribe.

The cave, which has only two other possible equals in Britain, at Denbigh and in Devon, is on the edge of a 180-foot quarry crater, where many Laugharne men are employed, and in it have been found remains of the mammoth, the woolly rhinoceros and cave lion, the hyena and traces of other prehistoric animals. These may be seen in the small County Museum in Quay Street, Carmarthen, together incidentally with a pair of cuff-links worn by Dylan Thomas!

Near the entrance to the cave is an aperture in the floor through which a room beneath has been discovered, but not yet explored. It has, however, been ascertained that there is yet another large cave. The roof, very low in some parts, was, until a few years ago, rich in stalactites, of which it was unfairly robbed. The floor is composed of what is thought to be the excrement of animals. In 1800 or 1810 was found a sacrificial censer or thuribulum of bronze, very highly finished, containing sixty coins of the period of the Roman Empire. Mr Kemp, an antiquarian, who wrote an account of Laugharne in the *Gentleman's Magazine* for 1839 and 1842, examined it and doubted the correctness of its discovery in a cave, thinking it more likely that it was found in excavating the limestone from the hill and that the coins were of the period of Carausius. In 1842 he says, quarry-men digging for stone on Coigan, found on its northern top the skeleton of an immense man, lying in a sort of cell cut in the rock. The tomb was 4½ feet in length, 2½ feet in breadth and 2 feet deep, but in parts its size varied. The skeleton lay on its side, with the head to the north, knees bent. This grave was sealed by a huge stone called a clegger, nearly circular, about 5 feet in diameter, 10 to 11 feet thick. Since it is solid limestone here it must have been brought from the adjoining hill, and that with great labour, showing, as Mr Kemp says, that there had been no secrecy about the burial. The top of the covering stone lay a foot below the surface of the earth, and around the edges of it a dry wall had been built. The whole grave was overgrown with turf, and quite concealed from view, till the opening being made at the side displayed the skeleton. This induced the excavators to remove the soil and turf from the top to see the size of the stone. The Rev. J. N. Harrison, Vicar of Laugharne, sent an account of this discovery to Mr Kemp:

> The position of the body indicates a very early period for the tomb, the most ancient mode of burial deposited the body within a cist, with the head to the North and the knees drawn up, which was an Eastern custom, and the method here of closing the aperture to the grave was a very ancient one.

The Coigan had long been known to the inhabitants of Laugharne, but never explored scientifically until the autumn of 1866, when Mr Allan and Mr Hicks of St Davids excavated it and found there bones and teeth of hyenas, hippopotami, rhinoceros, mammoth, red deer, the floor being strewn with fragments of bones. All the bones found then and afterwards were sent to Professor Boyd Dawkins, who said that 'The teeth indicate every variety from the whelp to the adult in the decline of life.'

In his speech to the Cambrian Archaeological Society meeting in Carmarthen, August 1875, Mr Allan said:

> This cave was an ancient hyena den; the bones introduced by hyenas are distinguished from those brought in by water or some other agency by their imperfect state, since all the eatable portions are gone, the hyenas have eaten all the eatable parts. The scanty herbage now on the bare hills near Laugharne would not provide nourishment enough for such gigantic animals, nor cover for them, so that there must have been a much larger area of pasturage when these animals perished than there is at present; hence geologists have inferred that there must have been an alteration of the level on the land, and that at the period we are speaking of, Coigan Rock overlooked a vast fertile plain affording abundant pasturage and occupying the present site of the Bristol Channel. The elevation of the district above its present level was part of the general elevation of the whole of Western Europe.

22

Illustration inspired by Coygen Cave, Laugharne

Painting of Druid sacrifice

Miss Curtis's sitting room, Laugharne

The second time he found bones here, Mr Allan sent them to the museum of Rugby School. Since this, others have explored the cave and found bones of the elephant, two teeth and bones of the bear and traces of elk, oxen and other animals.

The nineteenth century brought other researchers to Laugharne. A Miss Mary Curtis came from London as a governess. She rented a room in a small house in King Street, belonging to a family called Edwards, who were the local builders and undertakers. The house, which had once been a Post Office and a druggist's shop, still retains its character with an attractive bow front window. Miss Elizabeth Edwards, a lady in her seventies, who lives in the house with her bachelor brother Aubrey, remembers Mary Curtis living there, she says:

> Mary Curtis was a tiny woman who wore her hair parted in the middle and pulled severely back to the nape of the neck, Victorian style. She usually wore a long black dress and a lace fichu across her shoulders. She loved telling ghost stories and was a keen collector of wild flowers to press, and of seashells. During her stay in Laugharne she studied local history and wrote *The Antiquities of Laugharne and Pendine,* staying up most of the night writing, then going to bed when the household was asleep.

In her book which was published in 1880, Mary Curtis wrote:

> It has been an opinion assumed by many without due investigation, that The Welsh have not and do not attain a high standing in literature and science and are generally far below the English. This is untrue. At an early period when England's literary standard was very low, Wales was rich in poetry. Her Augustine age was 1100 to 1500. Thierry says: 'The Welsh of Middle Ages were the most intellectual people of Europe.'

Indeed, the most honoured guests at the Court of the Welsh Princes were bards (poets). Most of them composed and recited poems in praise of God, the Saints and the Princes of Wales. To become a bard one was apprenticed to an older bard and studied stories of Welsh heroes, saints and customs. Bards chanted poems while the Court feasted in the great halls. Wandering bards like wandering minstrels strolled the Welsh countryside and were welcomed by the poor and the rich, like actors during the last war, they helped to keep up the spirits and morale of the people, telling stories from the Mabinogion and praising their wealthy hosts who dined and wined them generously.

Mary Curtis could not know when she wrote her book, that Wales's greatest poet was yet to be born, and that he was to spend fifteen years of his short life in the Laugharne in which she herself lived and died. Miss Curtis dealt, however, with such local celebrities as Laugharne had already produced in her time. Thus, she mentions Dr Josiah Tucker, Dean of Gloucester, a distinguished scholar and divine and a political writer, who was born in Laugharne in 1713.

Of this cleric, Miss Burney, the authoress of Evelina, when in attendance on Queen Charlotte, had something to say in her diary when he visited the court of George III at

Fauconberg Hall, Cheltenham. She wrote: 'I was very glad to see him, he has a most shrewd, keen face and is past eighty;' His work *Cui Bono* was upon the impolicy of war.

Another worthy recalled by Miss Curtis, was the Rev. Peter Williams who was born on a farm on the Marsh, Laugharne, in 1721.

Although he was made a deacon by the Bishop of St Davids, and became curate of Eglwyscummin, an ancient church on the outskirts of Laugharne, he had 'methodistical principles' and was dismissed his post. He became successively curate at Swansea, Llangranog, Cardiganshire and at Llandysilio, but there again was dismissed for the same reasons.

Williams left the Church and joined the Methodists, but here too, his luck ran out. He was unjustly accused of heresy and expelled the Methodist Society in his seventieth year. He then joined the Independants. He died in 1796, but not before he had written his *Family Bible* published in 1770, and *Welsh Concordance of the Bible* published in 1773. In 1790, he published the Bible with Canne's marginal notes and references, with additional ones of his own, all in Welsh. His life is written in Rees's *History of Protestant Nonconformity in Wales*. The first edition of *Family Bible* can be seen at Eglwyscummin Church.

*   *   *   *

So famous has Laugharne always been for cockles, that even the portreeve's chain of office has links of gold cockleshells. Mary Curtis wrote:

> Malkin, who was in Laugharne in 1803, says it was the best built town in Carmarthenshire. It has improved in cleanliness, but not in buildings; Gosport, where the cockle people dwell, was a dirty place not fit to walk through; heaps of cockleshells were piled up against the houses; this is not allowed now.

During this century, the old corn wharf, now a ruin, became a cockle factory employing local labour. Now it is used for storage purposes and is due for demolition.

In 1756, Lady Maude Crowe of Westmead, Laugharne, tried to stop the Laugharne people from fishing in the open sea, then their only means of livelihood apart from agricultural work. She lost her case at the Quarter Sessions, where it was ruled that 'The sea is as free as the air'.

On the floor within the rails of St Martin's Church is the tombstone of this formidable lady, who died on March 27th, 1779, aged eighty-two. Her misleading epitaph reads:

> This Matrons wish through all her lengthened days
> Was not to captivate, but merit praise;
> With liberal hand and sympathising heart,
> To aid pale want, and blunt afflictions dart,
> As oft withdrawing from the great and gay,
> She sought the cot where meek misfortunes lay
> And would have kept each generous deed unknown,
> But mindful gratitude inscribed this stone.

Llanstephan sands

Min Lewis and Family, Llanstephen Sands

Marros Bay

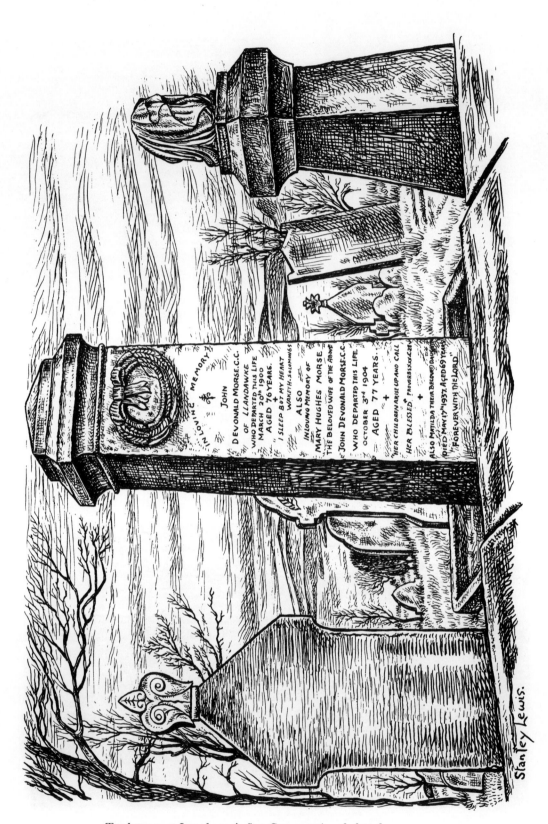

Tombstones at Laugharne's first Congregational chapel

Nearly a century later, in 1870, Mary Curtis stated:

The fishing trade is not so great a support to the labouring class as it was. In 1861, the liberty of fishing for salmon and sewin (grilse) was taken away with other advantages, by the Act which requires everyone to take out a licence. The right of taking all other kinds of fish is allowed. This has raised the price of salmon to 10 pence and one shilling and two pence and sewin to one shilling, which was before 3pence per pound. Their principal support is from flat-fish and cockles. The inhabitants of Laugharne have the liberty of fishing in the River Taf from St Clears to the sea and other parts where the estate of Westmead joins.

Flat-fish, locally called dabs, are easily speared since they are flat. A stabbing fork is used for this purpose; a long handled fork with barbed prongs at the end. A few Laugharne men still continue the tradition of gathering cockles for a livelihood, Elliot James and Tommy James go to the Llanstephan cockle beds. Elliot also lays nets to trap the fish from the incoming tides.

*   *   *   *

Dylan wrote:

But when you say in a nearby village or town, that you come from this unique, this waylaying, old lost Laugharne where some people start to retire before they start to work and where longish journeys of a few hundred yards are often undertaken on bicycles, then oh the wavy edging away the whispers and whimpers, and nudges, the swift removal of portable objects.

This was no joke, for it is perfectly true that Laugharne once had a bad reputation for quarrelling and fighting and the stigma is still there, although it is now a most peaceful and respectable community, being far less sinful, perhaps, than many of its chapel-bound neighbours. Only one Welsh chapel remains in Laugharne, the Congregational chapel in King Street, set back from the road and fenced in. It is well built and austere as most Welsh chapels are, but the congregation is so small that services are held there only once monthly. The harvest festival service is attended by all denominations, and the fruit, vegetables and flowers that decorate the chapel are auctioned at the end of the service.

Somehow the chapel has not flourished in Laugharne. The first Congregational chapel stood at the east end of Victoria Street, overlooking the bay on the way to the Cliff Walk and Dylan's house. Only the graveyard remains, with its interesting assortment of tombstones, for the chapel was sold and demolished and the pulpit used, of all things, to make the bar in the Brown's Hotel. The Wesleyan chapel, Newbridge Road, has been converted into a privately owned garage, while the Methodist chapel in Wogan Street was demolished and a public lavatory built on the foundation.

Miss Elizabeth Edwards told me that her grandmother went to the Quaker's chapel, which stood in Water Street and was demolished in the last century; she remembers her grandmother regularly attending the three chapel services on Sundays.

Two chapels remain on the outskirts of Laugharne, however, the Baptist chapel, Plashett, on the Pendine Road, and Bwllch Newydd, near St Clears.

In 1819, the Rev. David Davies was born at Cnwee Farm, Llanddowrot, and when he was fifteen he attended the evening classes held at Bwlchgwynt Chapel vestry; he eventually qualified as a road surveyor. At the age of twenty, David was baptised, and a year later began ,preaching at Bwlchgwynt Baptist Chapel. He was ordained in 1844, and soon became a fluent preacher in Welsh and English. He came to Laugharne and began preaching in a small house at Brook Hamlet, near Laugharne, but in a few years the congregation increased so rapidly that it was found necessary to build a chapel. A plot of land was presented by Mr Morgan of Brook Farm, and the first plans for a chapel were drawn up. Bethel Baptist Chapel, Plashett, Laugharne, was built in 1863, at a cost of £293.0.1½ , of which £215.0.1½ was collected by members. The Rev. David Davies continued to preach at Plashett for a number of years, until his health prevented him from taking an active part, and his death in 1878 deprived the chapel of its founder.

In 1872, a letter was sent to the Rev. Lewis Davies:

May 1872.

Dear Brother,

We as Baptist Churches at Bwlchnewydd and Bethel, Plashett, are in dire need of someone to Shepherd us in the Lord.

After listening to your preaching on several occasions, and that with great pleasure, also in full knowledge of your irreproachable character, after prayerful consideration of our circumstances we have come to a unanimous decision to invite you as our pastor, and as a successor to the Rev. David Davies.

We trust you will find it in your heart to comply with our request, and that the Lord will give you to us in the fullness of His Blessing.

We are not in a position at present to tell you what your stipend will be, but we make a solemn promise that we shall do our best for you.

On behalf of Bwlchnewydd,
Benjamin James, Jason Nichol and Lewis Evans.
On behalf of Bethel,
David Richards and James Richards, Deacons.

The Rev. Lewis Davies accepted the post and started a day school in the loft above the stable at Bwlchnewydd. Eager pupils flocked in, and the school extended to the vestry, but even that was too small for the number of children, and so in 1878, the Rev. Lewis Davies took over Minerva House in King Street, Laugharne. He retired in 1903, and died in 1907.

In May 1963, Plashett Baptist Chapel celebrated its centenary, and Douglas Rees, a postman, who was then a Deacon of the Chapel, told me that its numbers were decreasing rapidly. The chapel is neither prevalent nor dominant in Laugharne as it is in most other Welsh villages and towns. Marty Curtis writes:

Rees, in his *History of Nonconformity,* says:
The leaders of the Methodist movement in 1743 had never entertained the idea of setting up a new denomination. Their scheme was only intended to introduce and promote a revival of religion in the Established Church, but their measures being uncanonical, they were opposed by the dignitaries of the Church, and their attachment to the Establishment necessitated the nonconformists to keep aloof from them, in order to prevent the ruin of Nonconformity.

Most Welsh ministers, like Eli Jenkins in *Under Milk Wood,* put on a good show, with

Eli Jenkins and PC Attila Rees

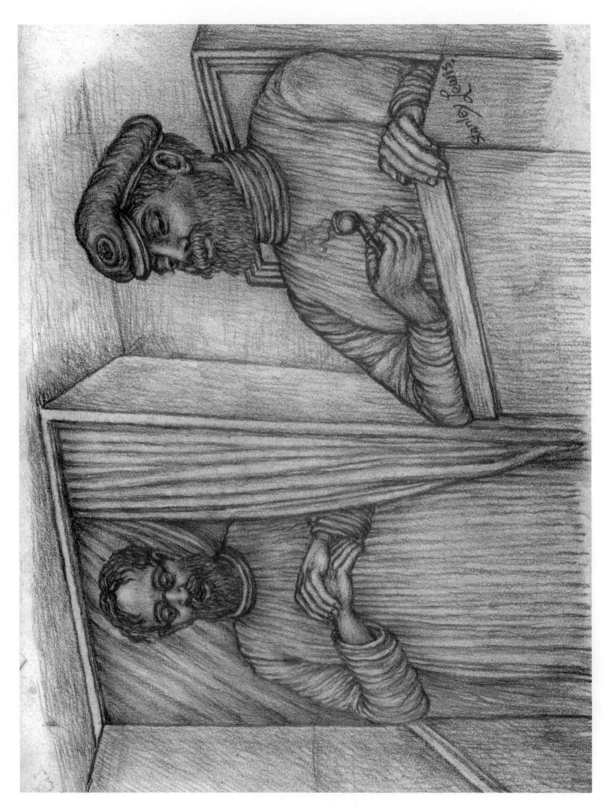

Captain Cat and Rev. Eli Jenkins, 1958

dramatic voices they emphasise their points in a God-fearing manner, that often puts the fear of God into the congregation; such ministers are referred to as 'Good Preachers'. The Welsh language with its lilting intonations helps them considerably. Many Welsh people will still travel far to hear a Good Preacher.

D. Parry Jones, in *Welsh Country Upbringing*, wrote on his introduction to religion in Wales:

> Everything went well for me until they began to preach. At first, fascinated by these robed ambassadors of another realm and sovereign, I mingled freely with the crowd until one of them got on to the subject of hell and punishment and began to expand in descriptive terms on the purpose and citizen-life of this nether region of the Prince of Wickedness. What in particular he said I have clean forgotten, but I can recall to this day the fact that he created a fear in my breast that utterly unnerved me.

And again:

> There was so much fire and brimstone, fear and punishment mixed up with it that I shall never forget the relief it was to me to grow out of childhood into the larger, emancipating knowledge of later teens and so escape from the fear and tyranny that gripped me. I pictured God as a hard, merciless schoolmaster able to see through my heart and mind, with an ineffaceable memory and an unlimited power over me. Undoubtedly I was an unusually sensitive and nervous child. My good mother never suspected the existence of my fears and agony of mind. Now I realise, of course, that all this agony was due to the way religion was presented to my generation. Yet the truth is that it fascinated me. I could not leave it alone.

The Cymanfa Ganu (Singing Festival) is a serious and great occasion for many chapel people. The usual Cymanfa Ganu is held every other year at the Methodist chapel called Moriah, at Llanstephan, when bus-loads of people dressed in new clothes and gay hats appear from every .part of the county to release their pent up emotions by singing. A mixed choir, singing traditional Welsh hymns, never fails to move my emotions, and is as much a part of Wales as its Sunday-closing pubs. Even so, nonconformity dams the true Welsh spirit by its severe doctrine, which to my mind is as austere and uninviting as the unimaginative box-like chapels. In the last century, eighty per cent of Wales was nonconformist; today, television has broadened the outlook of the younger people.

No doubt Dylan was fighting this strangling element all the time, for one feels impelled to shock such people who wear a sanctimonious expression as a clown wears a mask. In the story 'The Peaches', Dylan tells how his cousin Gwilym, dressed in minister's black, preached from a cart which served as his pulpit:

> Then he brought out his deepest voice again, and cried to the heavens and the bat-lined rafters and the hanging webs: 'Bless us this holy day, O Lord, bless me and Dylan and this Thy little chapel for ever and ever, Amen. I've done a lot of improvements to this place.'
> I sat on the hay and stared at Gwilym preaching, and heard his voice rise and crack and sink to a whisper and break into singing and Welsh and ring triumphantly and be wild and meek. The sun, through a hole, shone on his praying shoulders, and he

said: 'O God, Thou art everywhere all the time, in the dew of the morning, in the frost of the evening, in the field and the town, in the preacher and the sinner, in the sparrow and the big buzzard. Thou canst see everything, right down deep in our hearts; Thou canst see us when the sun is gone; Thou canst see us when there aren't any stars, in the gravy blackness, in the deep, deep, deep, deep pit; Thou canst see and spy and watch us all the time, in the little black corners, in the big cowboys' prairies, under the blankets when we're snoring fast, in the terrible shadows; pitch black, pitch black; Thou canst see everything we do, in the night and day, in the day and the night, everything, everything; Thou canst see all the time. O God, mun, you're like a bloody cat.'

Rhys Davies in *The Story of Wales*, described William Price of Llantrisant, an earlier rebel than Dylan:

He died, aged ninety-three, in 1893, and is known chiefly as the pioneer of cremation in Britain. But he also defied in most exhibitory fashion, the conventions and beliefs of his time, including law, religion, morality and his own medical profession. In his youth he practised nudism. Roaming stark naked the Victorian-clouded mountains about his home he attempted to bring back to them something of their old paganism. He hailed from a family of some consequence, his father was an ordained priest and he was a scholar. Calling himself a druid, this dignified adult named one of his sons Jesus Christ, and, in his public appearances, dressed in a succession of weird and highly coloured costumes, the most conspicuous item being a ruddy fox-skin head-dress, the tail and legs arranged about his shoulders. He preached 'free love' and was personally successful in this philosophy, and standing on a prehistoric stone in Pontypridd he would chant pagan addresses to the moors. His great talent as a physician earned him extra fame, but he vehemently attacked the medical superstitions of Victoria's reign. Stately in appearance, he never ate meat, his favourite drink was champagne and he was strong and handsome as an oak.

Dr Price was a rebellious Welshman who used showmanship as a means, to help his cause, for as Rhys Davies wrote: 'He saw the harm a mishandled religion could work in a people capable of a luminous gaiety.'

Being a Chapel Minister was an ideal profession in Wales, for the minister was respected almost as much as God, feasting fat on eggs, bacon and potatoes freely given to the Great Man by the small farmers who could ill afford to be generous. Perhaps it is good that nonconformity has not completely won its battle, for the Welshman has not yet lost his sense of humour.

Although the chapel has withered at Laugharne, the people are proud of their beautiful church, and generously support it on all occasions.

St Martin's Church, at the northern end of Laugharne, is set back from the road and approached through a lych-gate and a long drive hedged on both sides.

This church with its square tower, which was lowered in 1873, was probably erected by Sir Guy de Brian, Lord High Admiral to King Edward III of England in the French wars. The arms of Sir Guy de Brian, together with King Edward's head, are depicted in a stained glass window in the nave of the church.

A former portreeve of Laugharne, the late Alderman E. V. Williams, M.A., B.Litt.,

*Stanley in front of his Royal Academy painting of the
Cow Shed at Orchard House, Llansetephan*

Welsh Cow Shed in 1950

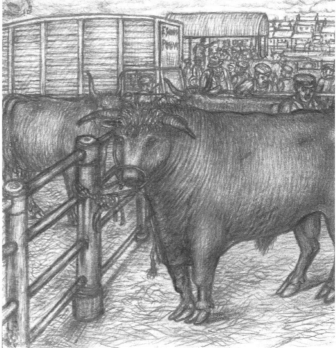

Carmarthen Cattle Market

Carmarthen Cattle Market

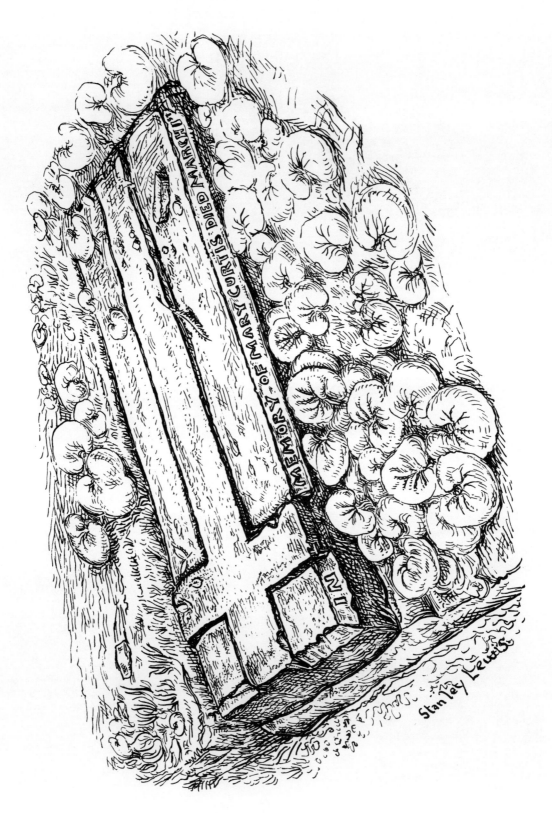

Mary Curtin's grave stone

was often besieged by visitors who asked to be directed to the memorial 'To Dylan Thomas.'

Many of these people, who had probably never read a line of Dylan's poetry, but had seen or heard *Under Milk Wood* performed, were unabashed when E. V. replied with his tongue in his cheek, 'This window is in memory of Sir Guy de Brian, founder of this church, and this one,' pointing to a window the other side, 'is in memory of Polly Garter.' Sometimes, E. V. Williams was bluntly asked whether he was the Organ Morgan caricatured by Dylan in *Under Milk Wood*. Amused by their impudence, he occasionally agreed he was.

On the north wall of the church is a wood-carving of Saint Martin casting his cloak, which came from Oberammergau, Bavaria, the home of the Passion Play.

On the south wall, near the entrance, is a large oil-painting of a saint, unsigned, but painted in the style of James Thornhill (1676-1734), the father-in-law of Hogarth, who was patronised by Queen Anne, and was commissioned to decorate the large hall of Greenwich, and some apartments in Hampton Court Palace. But perhaps his most famous work is in the dome of St Paul's Cathedral, London, where the principal events in St Paul's life are portrayed in eight frescoes.

A casket holding the remains of the bronze age Beaker Man, found while excavating at Orchard Park (now a Laugharne Council estate), lies on a shelf in the side chapel.

The church is surrounded by an interesting graveyard with tombs and graves on different levels, some still fenced in for fear of long-dead resurrectionists. The verses of the nineteenth-century graveyard poets are interesting to notice. One, marked 1864, reads as a warning:

> If thou at last to heav'n would go
> Mind how you lead your lives below,
> A life in sin and folly past,
> Can never lead to heaven at last.

In 1871, a dramatic epitaph was composed in memory of a sailor drowned on the barque *Daring:*

> Though Borea's blast and Neptune's waves
> Have tossed me to and fro
> 'Yet I at last by God's decrees
> Do harbour here below
> There at an anchor I do ride
> With many of our fleet
> Once more again I must set sail
> My Saviour Christ to meet.

A stone dated 1826, stands in memory of several babies, with the verse:

> They came the cup of Life to sip
> Too bitter it was to Drain
> They turned their little heads aside
> And went to sleep again.

37

The epitaph of a child in 1846 reads:

> This lovely Bird so young and fair
> Cut off in early doom,
> Just came to show how sweet a flower
> In Paradise could bloom.

And another in 1862 gives us all fair warning:

> My loving friend prepare to die
> For die, you must, like me
> And whether you're prepared or not,
> Death's sure to call for thee.

A local poet, sometimes called a graveyard poet, composed the memorial verses found in the village churchyards. His payment was probably very small.

In *Welsh Country Upbringing*, D. Parry Jones wrote:

A visit would be made (possibly anticipated) to the local poet, a poor working man of the name of Thomas, who laboured mostly on the farms, interspersed in his earlier years with periods in the Carmarthenshire coal mines.

This man who had composed memorial verses to practically all families in that district was entirely the product of the Sundayschool, the principal educational agency, especially in those days. His payment, if any, would be some commodity from the farm such as cheese, butter, a wheaten loaf, or perhaps the hauling of a load of coal.

I have read many of these elegies, which, though mournful in character following the fashion and imitating the sentiments of hymns then popular, were full of gospel comfort, of quite considerable, even respectable merit, showing an extensive vocabulary and a mastery of diction, rhythm and rhyme.

Besides old gravestones, there are also some fine old yew trees, but the main avenue of yew trees was blown down on to the church roof by an unusually fierce gale some years back. Parishioners subscribed generously, and in a short time enough money was collected for a new roof. Of these yew trees, Mary Curtis wrote:

In 1720, those yew trees which give so pleasing a shade and so venerable a look to the picturesque churchyard, were planted.

The old one near the church door in the south transept is called the 'Fox Tree', from the custom of hanging foxes' heads on it; Pole-cats and other animals were hung on it as well. In old times when it was a necessity to exterminate certain animals, as foxes, wolves, etc., a reward was given to those who captured them, and it was usual to attach their heads to the cross in the churchyard for the purpose of valuing them. They remained on the cross usually for three church services and after that the reward was given. For a wolf's head, the same sum was awarded as for the capture of the greatest robber; for foxes 2/6 and 1/6.

Water Meadows House with Min Lewis, St. Clears

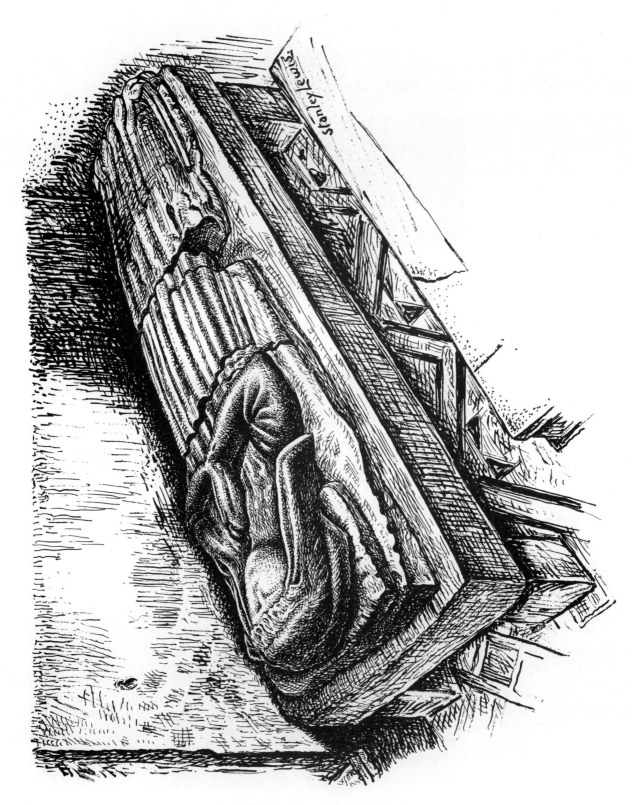

Probably the effigy of Margaret Marloes

In the Register of Laugharne Church stands this account of the rewards:

By the vestry held in May 1723, it was agreed that as there was a difference in the accustomed reward for destroying vermin there should be imposed on the Town, Marsh and Parish an allowance.

For every vixen fox, 6d., every dog fox, 1/-, every cub or young fox of either sex under a year old 1 /-, every badger, 6d., every wild-cat, 6d., every owl, 3d.

Signed: Thomas Phillips, Vicar.

It is a wonder that any wild animal survived those days, but the rewards fortunately did little to exterminate them, for, though there are no wild cats, foxes and badgers abound in the spinneys, and the owls' favourite haunts are the yew trees in the churchyard. The last wolf captured in Wales was said to have been caught not far from Tenby.

During the last century in isolated villages unlit except by oil-lamps and candles, superstition was rife, for life was shorter, more frightening and certainly much narrower than it now is. Then, it was the custom for a person to be appointed to go to church on All Hallows Eve to hear the names of those who would die within the year. In the diocese of St David's the belief then survived that, 'Lights travel the road by which the dead will be carried to burial.' Mary Curtis wrote of this superstition:

The funeral procession, too, is seen previously and the mourners distinctly recognised. One tradition says, they appear in answer to the prayer of St. Lanon. She desired that the people might be warned before death came and so have time to prepare themselves. Another says, it was in consequence of Bishop Ferrar, who was burnt at the stake in Carmarthen, declaring that if his doctrine was true, a light would go before the death of every person in the diocese of St. Davids.

About a mile and a quarter from Laugharne is Llandawke Church, dedicated to Saint Margaret Marloes or Marlos, and built in the thirteenth century.

Near the altar stands a stone effigy of a woman in a flowing gown and wearing a wimple. The stone is broken in three places, but it has been put together again, and the effigy is probably one of Margaret Marloes. There is also an Ogham stone with a Latin inscription.

A legend persists about the effigy of the lady cut in three which is said to represent the foundress of the church. She was supposed to have lived at Broadway, and one day as she was returning across Hugden, from arranging the business of Llandawke Church, robbers attacked her, and cut her into three parts. To commemorate her martyrdom, her effigy was divided into three parts and the church dedicated to her. There may be very little truth in this story and like many tales it is probably romanticised, but it is still cherished, as it was once the belief that Margaret Marloes's ghost often appeared on Llandawke land leading to the church. Another legend concerns a bride murdered at Llandawke on her wedding day and her body thrown into the pond behind the church, which she afterwards haunted. Her husband is said. to have been murdered at the same time although his body, which was found outside the church door, showed no signs of violence. The tenants of Rectory farm, which is next door to the church, have neither seen nor heard any unusual happenings.

Once a year, when the annual Harvest Festival is held at Llandawke, the farmers and their wives decorate the little church, to hide the dampness that is gradually destroying the walls, and although the winds blow through the broken windows, and there are chilling discomforts, the church returns to life with joyful voices accompanied by the old pedal organ. After the service, the fruit, corn, flowers and vegetables are sold by auction, since there is not enough produce to take to hospital, and no Sunday service follows the weekday festival.

* * * *

Once, there was a flourishing market in Laugharne. Held under the Town Hall every Friday, butter, eggs, poultry and meat were sold there. On other days of the week, meat was purchased from the farmers and publicans, for there were no butchers' shops in Laugharne formerly.

Mary Curtis wrote of this market:

On market day, the town was full, the farmers with their wives and daughters coming in from Llanboidy and other parts on horseback, seated on a sort of cushion, called a pannel, with large bags of striped woollen stuff, some full of corn, others of oats, swung on each side of the horse. ere would be perhaps sixty or seventy farmers in the town on this day. The corn and oats were sold to the different store-houses and were then regularly shipped for Bristol. This was the state of things about fifty years ago (1820). At this period, some of the pleasant scenes of country life were common in Laugharne.

The farm-maids would come into the town from the farms around every week with baskets of butter, some with poultry and eggs, themselves the perfection of neatness and cleanliness, wearing the Welsh hat and costume, their well frilled caps as white as snow, sometimes with bright ribbons fluttering in the wind. Though much of this is departed, there are still many coming in during the week. It is their holiday, they look to it with pleasure. The labouring people find great support from the sale of fish, especially of cockles. It is a busy scene, one fit for an artist, when the women come in from the sands with their bags of cockles, perhaps they have walked miles. They return as they went, in groups dressed in their worst, with hats of all sizes and shapes, generally with the well-known handkerchief tied over their heads; their skirts tucked up in all forms, some not unlike those of the fashionable ladies; wooden shoes, some with baskets, others with tinpans on their heads full of cockles, which they poise admirably with their arms akimbo, though one will put her hand to the load. Six or ten women will come in with six or more poor donkeys, staggering under their loads, one or two happy to have only one bag across his back, others will have two or even three. On Sundays, these women come out like butterflies dressed in all their finery.

When farmers came in with corn, two toll gatherers, Molly Richard and Sally Lewis, would stand, one by Mariner's corner, the other by the storehouse on the Grist, holding a wooden dish to receive the toll. One dish of each kind of grain out of every sack was required, the half of what was in the dish went to the Portreeve of the town, the other half to the women who received the toll.

The Rebecca riots ended the tolls, and for more than half a century the market was not used. A few years ago, it was reopened by the Women's Institute, the toll, a penny in the shilling for all goods sold. Home-produced things only are allowed to be sold. There is a table laden with fruit cakes, tarts, and sponge cakes rich with cream. Another table is reserved for bunches of mint and parsley, sour rhubarb and home preserved jams,

Llandawke Church

The Old Bell in St. Peter's Church, Carmarthen

School children and teachers in the rain, waiting for a bus in Llamas Street, Carmarthen

marked lemon marmalade and orange, blackberry jelly and lemon curd, pickles and jars of tomato and apple chutney. Seedling plants grown in wooden boxes to sell at 4d. a piece, cabbages and beans, flowers and frowns and plenty of fuss. The same familiar faithfuls come and buy in the early hours of Saturday morning, bidding each other a frosty good hunting in the draughty prison-like market. 'Five shillings for that cake,' said one disgruntled shopper, 'I can make it for half that price at home!'

When the rush of customers is gone, the sellers, beaming from their busy half-hour, rub their hands and stamp their feet and shiver in the draughty room like dabs on marble slabs, but the individuality of the market is gone. It is no longer a country market in the true sense of the word, selling poultry and meat, fresh eggs and home-made butter and cheese. Laugharne has lost its picturesque market as surely as it has lost its webbed-foot women and its boozing poet.

Another type of market flourished in the neighbourhood of Laugharne and Carmarthen during the last war, bringing prosperity to many a previously hard-up small farm, for the black-market flourished despite the fear of Ministry Inspectors who might, like the Gestapo, call at any time.

The war gave rise to amusing and vivid stories, of the entrails of illegally slaughtered sheep buried in hayricks, until the smell eventually aroused suspicion. Of pigs slaughtered without licence, the carcases fetching high prices on the black-market. There was a story of an inspector calling at a farmhouse to search for illegally slaughtered meat, but the farmer outwitted the inspector by hiding the sides of bacon and hams in bed with his wife assuring the inspector in all innocence that his wife was ill with a contagious complaint. Suspicious as he was, the inspector did not have the nerve to search the bed, so the meat was not discovered. There are many more tales told of an inspector outdone by a dumb-cluck farmer, but the farmers did not always get away with it.

However, even the humble, despised rabbit enriched many of them, and they were handsomely subsidised by the government.

Carmarthen would be a very poor town without the patronage of the farmers who flock to the market on market days and freely spend their money.

To attract the farmers, the public houses remain open all day, friendly crowds gather there, and it is amusingly said that more deals are made in the pubs than in the market itself. Wednesday and Saturday are the chief market days, but any cattle sale is sufficient excuse for the pubs of Carmarthen to remain open, so Carmarthen of all places, is a boozer's paradise! To honour the farmers who visit them, most of the pubs have fitting names, the Drovers, the Red Cow, the Tanners Arms, to mention a few.

Wednesday is the busiest day in the cattle market, when farmers from remote parts of the county bring in their cows, calves, sheep and pigs for the auctioneer to sell under the hammer. The market is a hive of activity, loud with shouting voices and noises of plaintive moos, baas and the squealing of pigs. A. G. Bradley wrote in his *Highways and Byways in South Wales:*

A cheerier or more bustling agricultural centre on its two weekly market days or monthly fair could not be found in all Great Britain.

A sturdy, rosy, good-humoured and apparently light-hearted crowd it is too, that swarms about the serried ranks of carts in the byways adjoining the spacious marketplace.

Many farmers and their sons who spend hard lonely lives on isolated farms often drink more than enough on fair and market days, mostly because the pubs are a meeting place for friends.

The tidal River Towy flows through Carmarthen, and during the salmon season the Towy fishermen with their coracles on their backs, looking for all the world like gigantic black beetles, are a familiar sight. The coracle, which is made by the fishermen, is a small oval flat-bottomed boat consisting of tarred canvas stretched over a willow or hazelwood frame of interwoven rods. Since it weighs no more than thirty pounds it is light enough to carry on a man's back. Coracle men work in pairs, each holding a side of the net as they sweep the river for sewin or salmon. When a coracle is too old to be used, it is usually burnt, a custom probably arising from an ancient rite wherein coracles were sacrificed to the river gods. Coracles pass the door of my home on the bank of the River Taf at St Clears.

On the right side of the banks of the River Towy is Llangunnor village, famous for its literary associations. Sir Richard Steele, soldier, and one of the first British journalists, who married Mary Scurlock of Ty-Gwyn, lived there. Together with Joseph Addison, he founded the *Tatler* in 1709, and then the *Spectator* and the *Guardian*. Lady Steele was buried in Westminster Abbey, but Richard Steele was buried in St Peter's Church, Carmarthen. Of him, Dean Swift wrote:

> Thus Steele who owned what others writ
> And flourished by imputed wit
> From perils of a hundred jayls
> Withdrew to starve and dye in Wales.

The following century, Sir Lewis Morris, poet and friend of Tennyson, died and was buried at Llangunnor in accordance with a wish expressed in a poem years before:

> Let me at last be laid
> On that hillside I know, which scans the vale
> Beneath the thick yew's shade
> For shelter when the rains and winds prevail.

Of other men worthy of note is the Welsh hymnologist, David Charles, also buried at Llangunnor.

On March 30th, 1555, in the reign of the Roman Catholic, Queen Mary, Robert Ferrar, the first Protestant Bishop of St David's, was burnt at the stake in Nott Square, Carmarthen. The stone in which the stake was fixed now forms the apex of Abergwili Church spire.

A familiar Carmarthen landmark which once was shown on the television programme, 'Stranger than Fiction', is the old Merlin Oak in Priory Street. This old, rotten, unrecognisable tree trunk now looking like a piece of modern sculpture, is held together by concrete and protected by iron railings. Situated in an awkward and dangerous part of the road, it has proved a costly monument to maintain. Are the Carmarthen people superstitious? Do they feel that Merlin's prophecy,

> When Merlin's tree shall tumble down
> Then shall fall Carmarthen town

CARMARTHEN
SCHOOL OF ART
1956-57

Merlin's Oak, Priory Street, Carmarthen

Welsh Costume

is perhaps true and are afraid to tempt Providence? The fated day was prophesied as Lammas Day, and years ago many people left the town on that day for fear they would perish when the town was flooded.

* * * *

Once, the accepted reply to the question, 'What are the chief products of Wales?' was 'Flannel to clothe, cheese to feed and sermons to take one to Heaven.'

The attractive Welsh cloth woven at the many small mills from Abergwili to Llandyssul to Newcastle Emlyn, is now widely known. Used for modern suits and coats, it is exported and admired at fashion-shows all over Europe. The gaily-coloured Welsh blankets and bedspreads woven in a tapestry design, are sold in the markets of Carmarthen, Tenby and Cardigan.

Once the cloth was used for the traditional Welsh costume, now only worn by Welsh children on March 1st, which is Saint David's Day. In 1879, Mary Curtis wrote about the changing fashion of dress:

> The Welsh costume is fast going out and the ugly fashion of the day taking its place. It is now only worn by elderly people, and not always by them; when they depart there will be an end of it.

The costume worn at Laugharne and throughout Carmarthenshire, consisted of a petticoat, probably made of merino, and a woollen shawl. The woollen material was called ninco, a coarse worsted yarn whose colour varied in the various counties. In Carmarthenshire, it was black, brown, dark blue or wine colour, and the pattern was striped. The woollen shawl was fastened with thorn pins (thorns from the thorn tree sharpened and dried by the fire). Sometimes a muslin or silk handkerchief, fastened with a brooch or gold-pin was used to cover the neck.

With passing centuries, not only have the fashions of clothes changed, but Welsh customs too. Weddings are no longer as colourful and gay as they formerly were. Of these weddings, Mary Curtis wrote:

> The customs at weddings were very curious in Wales. On the wedding day the bridegroom would send a friend, attended with twelve more of his friends, perhaps thirty or forty, to the bride's house to bring her to the church, or he might come himself. When arrived at the door, they found it bolted; the friend or the bridegroom knocked and explained his errand, putting it in the form of verse. After a while, a window above would be opened, and a male relative of the bride or some other person appeared and asked in verse what he wanted. He replied in verse, demanding the bride; this was stoutly refused. After some persuasion he got the door opened, and was let in. He had now to search for her, as she hid herself. The friend whose business it was to find her was called Gwyr, i.e. in English 'Seek out'. He placed her when found on his horse behind him, or on a horse by herself, and ran with her, galloping as hard as he could, for the bridegroom was not in possession yet. They gave her the first start; then the bridegroom and his friends tore after her. A hard race it was;

all were quite spent, and she yielded herself up Sometimes the bride and her relatives would be already mounted on horseback when the bridegroom and his friends arrived. They positively refused him the bride, upon which a mock scuffle ensued, while the bride, seating herself behind her next kinsman, is carried off, pursued by the other party with loud shouts, at full speed, 'crossing and jostling to the no small amusement of the spectators'.

'When they have fatigued themselves and their horses, the bridegroom is allowed to overtake his bride; he leads her away in triumph. They conclude with feasting and festivity.'

At local weddings, the tradition of 'holding the rope' still exists, surviving from centuries when children were not as well off as they are today. Village children hold a rope across the road to stop the bride and bridegroom's car, as they go and return from church. The rope is only lowered to allow them to pass when money has been thrown out. Then there is a terrific scramble as the children fight for the sixpences and threepenny pieces.

Even today in some remote villages, the custom of firing a shotgun when the bride leaves the house is kept up.

There were also unusual Welsh courting customs: Secretive in every respect, a Welsh lover would court his prospective bride when members 'of her household had retired for the night. Awakening her from sleep by throwing pebbles at her bedroom window, he would beckon her to let him in. If she accepted his advances she would silently creep downstairs to open the door. Then he would spend part of the night with her in the warmth of the kitchen. Instead of presenting her with an engagement ring, he would carve a spoon out of wood to present to his betrothed. The commonly used word 'spooning' is derived from this ancient Welsh custom.

Customs and nonconformity die hard, and even today in many parts of Wales, women are ashamed to enter public houses, for fear of being talked about, for gossip is scathing and does tremendous harm. It is still very much a man's world in Wales.

Dylan wrote:

Captain Cat: Can't hear what the women are gabbing round the pump. Same as ever. Who's having a baby, who blacked whose eye, seen Polly Garter giving her belly an airing, there should be a law, seen Mrs Beynon's new mauve jumper, it's her old grey jumper dyed, who's dead, who's dying, there's a lovely day, oh the cost of soap flakes!

Cruel gossip, harmful gossip, but the gossip of today is usually forgotten by tomorrow, there is always something happening, some interesting news to be enjoyed and talked over. Someone to console and someone to condemn. As a local saying avers: 'While they are talking about me, someone else is having a rest.' The Laugharne people seldom hold bitterness towards each other, and every tale is told with a smile; they are not as hypocritical as many of their neighbours, for happy-go-lucky Laugharne is not concerned about the faults of others, having as Dylan wrote: 'So many ripe and piping of its own.'

Polly Garter, Nogood Boyo and Mr Beynon

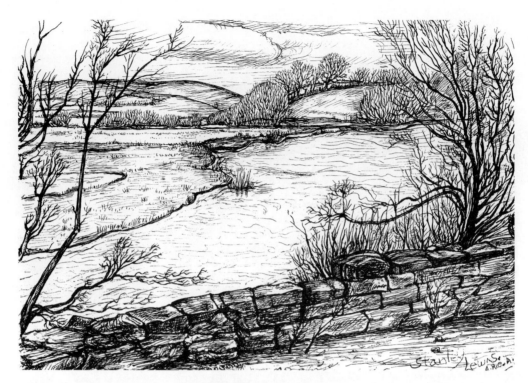

The River Dewi Fawr, St. Clears

Gosport Street, Laugharne

Perhaps that is why Dylan chose to live for fifteen years in this beautiful, barmy (both spellings) town.

Only a few miles away is St Clears, but the contrast in life and death is great; the epitaph on a stone set in the wall of St Mary's Church there, clearly indicates this. 'In memory of a man and his wife who both died in their 59th year leaving to their family an unspotted name.

Perhaps Laugharne treasures its traditions and picturesque sense of the past more than most Welsh towns and villages and so remains unique.

An attractive feature of Laugharne, are the cherry trees growing along the main street; but the blossoms blown into the houses by blustery winds caused annoyance to the house-holders, so they were badly pruned a few years ago and will not again blossom so profusely.

Dylan refers to the cherry trees growing in Coronation Street in *Under Milk Wood*, when he wrote:

> The main street, Coronation Street, consists, for the most part, of humble, two-storied houses many of which attempt to achieve some measure of gaiety by prinking themselves out in crude colours and by the liberal use of pinkwash, though there are remaining a few eighteenth-century houses of more pretension, if, on the whole, in a sad state of disrepair.

He could have been describing Laugharne, for the main Laugharne thoroughfare does indeed consist of humble two-storied houses pinkwashed and whitewashed; but the more pretentious eighteenth-century houses are now in a fairly good state of repair, since property has doubled in value.

Dylan continued:

> Though there is little to attract the hillclimber, the healthseeker, the sportsman, or the weekending motorist, the contemplative may, if sufficiently attracted to spare it some leisurely hours, find, in its cobbled streets and its little fishing harbour, in its several curious customs, and in the conversation of its local 'characters', some of that picturesque sense of the past so frequently lacking in towns and villages which have kept more abreast of the times. The River Dewi is said to abound in trout, but is much poached. The one place of worship, with its neglected graveyard, is of no architectural interest.

The River Dewi Fawr is a tributary of the River Taf, and flows through Upper St Clears. This river is popular with fishermen because of the abundance of trout.

Mary Curtis commented on the fact that Laugharne had not those interesting accessories such as the barber's shop with its long pole, nor a blacksmith's shop at the corner of a shady lane with an ancient oak or a noble horse-chestnut tree forming a leafy roof, but she recompenses this by writing:

> But it has features of greater interest than these, such as its antique ruins and natural beauties. In the locality called Gosport, are many ancient unpretending cottages, several with thatched roofs; some will have on the window frame two or three apples, perhaps a long row of them, long sticks perched upright to entice the little ones, often a solitary roll or a bun.

At eventide in the window a lonely candle makes visible these delights of the children, and. casts a narrow strip of light across the pathway. Laugharne has not lost its natural beauty, its position amid the hills, its picturesque churchyard, its pretty walks, its sheltered site on the edge of a small bay with the prospect of the prettiest line of coast imaginable. The New Walk, winding along the side of Sir John's Hill, affords a fine prospect. The old church of Saint Ishmael's seems to stand on the sea; the coast near Llanelly with a slight tint of green revealed by the gleam of the sun, its white habitations sprinkled about as pearls on a vesture of green; the Glamorganshire coast with its undulations so well wooded, its cliffs sparkling with the sunlight at the hour of a fine sunset; and Worm's Head. Here you can sit and see the vessels sailing down the Towy, perhaps the Tenby steamer from Carmarthen, or through your glass, a large barque well laden near Worm's Head, bound for the West, and numerous little vessels always passing to and fro. If the tide be out, a large piece of sand near the ferry looks beautiful, touched with the golden light of the sun.

If you come to this walk in autumn, 'When the streams come home' as the expression is with the people of these parts, your ear will be pleased and soothed by the gentle music of the many rills that gush out from the sides of the hill.

Laugharne has not changed greatly since those days. There are no longer thatched cottages at the Grist, nor do candles light the houses, neither does the Tenby steamer sail to Carmarthen, but the landscape is the same as it was when Mary Curtis saw and wrote about it. There was however a blacksmith in Laugharne then, as there is today. In those days Frederick Williams was blacksmith like his father and grandfather before him; in fact this remarkable family had been blacksmiths in Laugharne for generations.

Frederick, the son of John Williams, was born in 1830, and held the position of Common Attorney from 1883-1884. He was a typical Welshman, sturdy and strong, with a black beard, and many fine examples of his work can be seen in St Martin's Church. He was also much called for as a local singer, and when the choirmaster, Samuel David, was drowned in a boating accident in Laugharne, Frederick took over his job. Rules of the choir were strict in those days:

1. Members of the choir to be as regular as possible in their attendance both at the services of the Church and at the practising.
2. All members are to behave decently and devoutly in Church, to kneel in prayer and make all responses decently and reverentially.
3. All members are to attend at least one of the Choral Celebrations of Holy Communion in every month.
4. All male members of the Choir are to take part in the processions in Festivals. All female members are to be in their proper places before the procession enters the Church.
5. Adult members will receive their Christmas rewards in proportion to their attendance at the services and practising. Members unavoidably absent are expected to explain the cause of their absence to the Vicar or choirmaster.
6. All members are expected to be in their proper places some few minutes before the commencement of Service.
7. No one can be recognised as a member without signing these rules.

The Grist, Laugharne

Rebecca Riots

Frederick Williams married Jane David in 1856. There were ten children of the marriage, and the eldest son, Charles Williams (1862-1937), became a skilled musician who went to London and worked hard to get an orchestra together. His ambition was realised and he began a successful career as a conductor. Williams conducted the London Symphony Orchestra at the Queen's Hall, and the Berlin Philharmonic Orchestra in Berlin in 1906. His brother Arthur was soloist at the first performance. Another brother, David Williams (1869-1938), had no public career, but was a fine music teacher. Arthur Williams (1875-1939), who made his name in Germany before the First World War, was a brilliant cellist and was one of the German Klingter Quartet, which achieved its first outstanding success at the Beethoven Music Festival in Bonn. Unfortunately the war shortened his career in Germany. His wife Gwen was a fine pianist.

*   *   *   *

About four miles from Laugharne on the road to Carmarthen, is the small market place of St Clears, where, in the year 1843, the headquarters of the Rebecca rioters was situated.

The male leader of the rioters was called 'Rebecca' taken from a verse in Genesis: 'And they blessed Rebekah, and said unto her. Thou art our sister, be thou the mother of thousands of millions, and let thy seed possess the gate of those which hate them.' The raiders, consisting of an assortment of men, mainly farmers and farm labourers, dressed up in women's attire, and brandishing agricultural tools destroyed the toll gates and turnpike houses whose charges were extortionate. A rehearsed ritual was performed each time the rebels reached the toll gates. In Welsh the leader would ask:

'I cannot go on my daughters, there is something in my way. What is it?'
To which the rioters would reply: 'It's a toll gate, mother.'
'Has this turnpike any business to be here, my children?'
'NO.'
'Then what shall we do with it?'
'We must tear it down.'

The toll gate would be torn down (but no toll gates were destroyed on Sundays). The rebels grew in numbers, and the practice spread until the toll gates were abolished.

An insertion in the *Carmarthen Journal* at that period stated:

The Last of the Rebeccas.
Henry Evans committed to the county gaol September 3rd 1844 for being engaged in some of the Rebecca disturbances, and tried in March 1845 and sentenced to 18 months imprisonment, was discharged on Monday last, the period of his imprisonment having expired. He was the last of those unfortunate persons who were committed for various terms of imprisonment on account of their connection with Rebeccaism. When he entered the gaol he was not able to speak a word of English, nor did he know his alphabet, but when he was discharged he could speak English fluently, and was able to read the Bible, and repeated to the chaplin who expressed great satisfaction at his progress, the third chapter of Matthew, which he learned.

Not many miles from St Clears, is the ancient ruin of the Pilgrims' Church dedicated to St Michael and built on the banks of the River Cowyn. It has been a ruin for many years

57

and was probably a Norman structure. Pilgrims on the way to St David's Cathedral, Pembrokeshire, are said to have died and been buried there. Mary Curtis wrote of these graves:

> Tradition says three holy palmers, meeting here in great destitution, prepared for themselves three graves, agreeing that two of them should be put to death, the third, after burying them, was to lie down in the remaining grave and pull a large stone over it.

> On one gravestone is carved a coil of rope, on the second a hatchet and saw, on the third the figure of a woman with a ring on her finger. There are more gravestones besides these, but they are mostly overgrown with tall grass. The three pilgrim's monuments are considered to be the most valuable in Wales. A legend attached to the Pilgrims' graves states, that so long as the graves are respected by the public, Llanfihangel Abercowin will be free from poisonous snakes.

To reach the church, there is a pleasant walk through Trefenty farmyard and across two fields. Once a year, on the last Sunday in July, a service is held in the ruin, the transport being provided by Mrs Tudor Williams of Laugharne, whose father was vicar of the parish.

The Rev T. Charles, founder of the Bible Society, was born at the farmhouse of Pantdovan in the Parish of Llanfihangel.

*   *   *   *

A famous place, five miles from Laugharne, is Pendine, a village with miles of sands made famous by the late Sir Malcolm Campbell and Mr Parry Thomas when they attempted to break the motor speed record.

It was the starting point of Amy Johnson and Jim Mollison when they flew the Atlantic in July 1933.

Motor cycle speed championship races were held there, and it was a universal opinion that Pendine sands were the finest racing track in the country. Now the greater part of the sands have been requisitioned by a Government Experimental Establishment, which provides work for most of the people at Laugharne and surrounding districts.

*   *   *   *

Many of the elderly people of Laugharne remember the years when life was not as pleasant as it is now. Then an overbearing type of local aristocrat ruled Laugharne, treating the poorer people as serfs. Children were forced to curtsey when confronted by them and anyone who sat in the family's pews in church was severely reprimanded or removed. People were forced to walk on the road when the local aristocrat walked the pavement. How fortunate it is that these tyrants have had their day.

It was once the custom in Laugharne to have a football match through the town on Shrove Tuesday. The ball was called the 'Head of John the Baptist' and was a bladder covered by strips of leather. This game gave the locals the chance to take revenge on the people who displeased them. The game was so rough that every house was barricaded

58

Pendine Sands

Llanstephan Sands

Rev. Eli Jenkins

Fanny Brown, Cockle Picker

Characters in Under Milk Wood by the Llaregyb Players, 1958

and shuttered. Fighting became so frequent and frightening and so many were injured that in 1838, the magistrates banned the game for all time.

A funeral is a great occasion in most villages when mysterious Death is reverenced. Edmund Vale in his book, *How to See England,* wrote of the Welsh:

> A Welshman thinks more of the dead than of the living. No matter how shabbily you have lived, you will be respected in Wales when you have become a corpse. Yet it is not the corpse but the panoply of death which fascinates the Welshman as it seems to have done the people of the Stone Age.

The bigger the funeral the more respected the corpse is; it is a kind of prestige. Then black serge suits are brought out from mothballs and faces wear the expressions to suit the occasion. The corpse is laid out in the front parlour, a room which usually smells of damp and has several biblical texts on the patched walls or glass-painted saints.

The Welsh parlour is polished and only used on festival or funeral days. Then neighbours troop in to see the corpse before the lid is finally sealed. They remark on the peacefulness and beauty of the corpse's face, and then extol the deceased's virtues for hour after hour. Each family in the community sends at least one representative to the funeral.

Many years ago, a vigil was kept by neighbours until the funeral. Before the coffin is carried out, there is a short service at the house, and sometimes a Welsh hymn is sung. After the funeral, relatives and friends return to the house for a meal, while the male representatives usually adjourn to the nearest pub for refreshment.

The day of a man's funeral is the day when his reputation is at stake. A small funeral is damning, a large funeral the greatest honour a Welshman can hope for.

FRIENDS AND NEIGHBOURS

Not so many years ago, Laugharne was lit by candles and oil lamps as it was when Mary Curtis lived there, that is until Billy Williams, a former portreeve, produced an electricity plant, and was busily employed wiring the small cottages and the bigger houses of the township.

The Second World War had been declared a few months, when Mrs Richard Hughes organised an entertainment at the Memorial Hall, in aid of the Red Cross. A one-act farce called *The Devil Among the Skins,* written by Ernest Goodwin, was produced, with Dylan playing the part of the Tanner.

Laugharne Memorial Hall is, alas, an ugly building which through a mistake of the builder was erected back to front, so that the ugliest part faces the main road. The more attractive stone structure of the front faces the emerald green uprising field called Holloway, and a stream which is often occupied by ducks and moorhens flows past the door. The hall is a good hideout for mice who are rarely disturbed.

An entertainment was a welcome attraction in an isolated small township that had no theatre, no television and the nearest cinema thirteen miles away in Carmarthen town.

On December 18th, 1939, the Laugharne locals queued up outside the hall, rubbing their hands and stamping their feet as they waited for the door to be opened. Caitlin Thomas was selling programmes when Billy Williams, who had had the exacting job of arranging the stage lighting, asked her jokingly, 'How much did you take Cait?'

'Enough for us to have a booze up,' was her prompt reply.

Mrs Richard Hughes was the heroine in the piece. Her dress was made from several blue linen bedcovers, which Mrs Billy Williams made up into a laced up, full sweeping dress, with big sleeves. Don Davies, a tiny man from Victoria Street, played her lover. In one of the scenes he was supposed to put her across his knees and smack her, but Don Davies, who was much shorter than Mrs Hughes, was too shy to do this during rehearsals, although he did pluck up sufficient courage on the big night.

The play was a success and the cast and Billy Williams ('The Lights') were invited to the castle for supper afterwards. He recalls that the first course, cockle soup, was simply a bowl of salt water, with a solitary cockle floating on top. Then, to Billy's dismay, an enormous home-made meat pie with one slice missing that had played a prominent part in the play and sat in the hall throughout the previous week of rehearsals- appeared as the second course.

Of all the dinners and suppers Billy Williams has eaten in his lifetime, he remembers best the cockle soup and the great meat pie, for when he told me the tale, the tears ran down his cheeks and he chuckled with laughter at the thought of the mice who had partaken of the supper first!

Perhaps The Devil Among the Skins laughed too.

Mr William Watts, draper of Gwalia, knew Dylan as a family man concerned about his children's welfare. His elder son Llewellyn, was obviously damp-shod when Dylan wrote:

62

Gwalor House

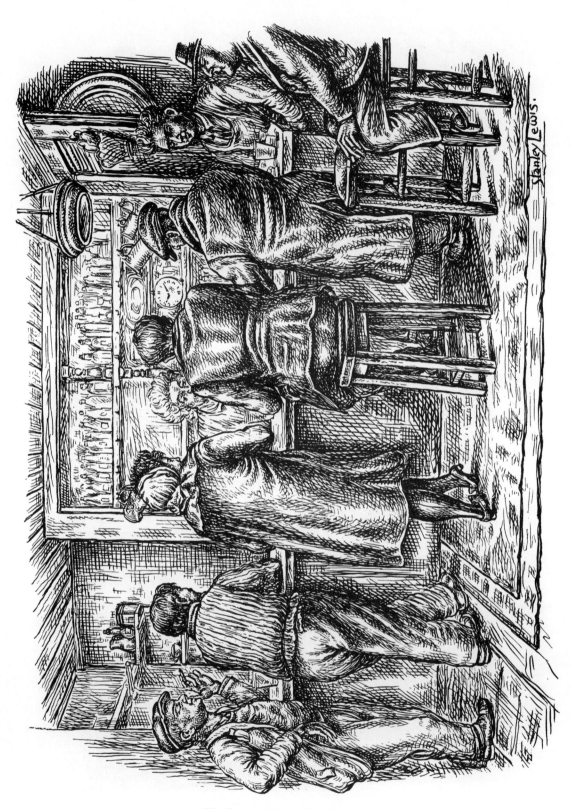

The Farmers Arms, Laugharne

Dear Mr Watts,

Will you please see that Llewellyn. buys a pair of wellington boots that fit him properly? I will be up later to settle with you.

Thank you,

Yours sincerely,

Dylan Thomas.

The late Mr William Watts's daughter, Mrs Gwen Jones, says of her father, 'Dada always wore a straw hat, a butterfly collar and a bow tie; he was very particular about his dress.' Dylan clearly modelled the clothing for his character Mr Edwards, draper, of Manchester House, in *Under Milk Wood,* from Mr Watts.

Mrs Jones recalls that the morning Dylan left Laugharne for his last trip to America, she walked along the cliff to enjoy the early morning air, and noticed the lane outside Dylan's workshed littered with tiny fragments of paper, each bearing a few words of poetry written in Dylan's recognisable handwriting, but it was impossible to glue the pieces together again and now they are lost.

Dylan frequented the Cross House. on the Grist, enjoying the company of Phillip Richards, landlord, and Romaine his daughter. He also visited the Corporation Arms, Gosport Street, to chat to Fleming Williams and his wife, and of course he was a 'regular' at the Brown's Hotel, King Street, where he chatted to Ivy and Ebbie Williams. Occasionally he called at other pubs.

Miss Annie Jeremy, who is nearly eighty and was the licensee of the Farmers' Arms, Church Street, until it was closed this year, told me of Dylan's infrequent visits.

'He only drank beer,' she said. 'He rarely spoke much and was always respectful.'

Perhaps Dylan wanted to hide his more boisterous moods from the people with whom he lived. Did he value their respect so much? Caitlin wrote 'There was a very strong puritanical streak in him, that his friends never suspected, but of which I got the disapproving benefit.'

He was not particular about his dress, always wearing unshapely baggy trousers like a tramp or maybe a clown. He never spoke about his work or indicated in any way that he was a poet, yet his shy reserved manner enabled him to observe the local characters shrewdly.

Dylan refers to 'The St Bernard without any brandy,' in his Laugharne story from *Early One Morning.* This giant dog belonged to Colonel Wilson, a rich retired army doctor, who bought one of Laugharne's biggest houses on the cliff, called Glan-y-Mor, which overlooks the Boat House and has a commanding view of the bay. The St Bernard was an enormous dog called Sam, who terrorised the town. In the words of Mrs Tudor Williams, 'He was a rogue-dog.'

Colonel Wilson spent £200 on fencing in his property to keep Sam from straying, yet a week after it was installed Sam jumped the fence and confronted Mrs Williams, who was taking her small Welsh corgi for a walk on the cliff. In fear, and trembling with emotion, she called to Dai Roberts 'the fish' who was terrified of dogs and always kept titbits in his pocket in case he was confronted by them.

'Please come and help me Dai Roberts,' she shouted, but Dai, who was hiding safely behind Dylan's gate leading to the Boat House, replied simply, 'Are you alright, Mrs Williams? I can't help you.'

She then called to Tom Adams, the gardener of Glan-y-Mor who had lumbago. 'If he kills you I can't come,' was Tom Adams's prompt and painful reply.

Sam was eventually lured to his right side of the fence, and Dai Roberts, still trembling with fear, emerged from the safety of Dylan's gate, and turning to Tom Adams, the gardener, said in all sincerity: 'I fort my end 'ad come, Tommy!'

Emrys Hughes, the postman, who had the job of collecting Sam's weekly ration of one hundredweight of Spratt's dog biscuits, remembers the day when he was given a different brand of biscuits because Spratt's were not in stock. Without hesitating, Emrys emptied the biscuits into the Spratt bag and delivered them as usual. When next he visited Glan-y-Mor, Colonel Wilson said quite seriously, 'Sam did not like those biscuits, I don't think they were Spratt's!'

Tradesmen trembled as they heeded the warning on the big iron gates, 'BEWARE OF THE DOG', and looked for a suitable and easy drainpipe to climb as soon as they reached the front door. 'Them sort of dogs are supposed to 'ave a bottle of brandy 'anging round their neck,' said one man. 'But if I saw one of them coming to my 'elp, I'd die of shock!'

When Sam escaped from Glan-y-Mor and the fateful words, 'Sam is coming', reached Victoria Street, everyone would beat a hasty retreat and cower behind locked doors, although they need not have feared, for Sam was well fed. Twice a week Colonel Wilson went to Abergwili on the outskirts of Carmarthen, to buy him horsemeat.

Not everyone was afraid of Sam, however. One summer, a little boy called Adamson, who was staying at Glan-y-Mor, painted Sam with blue paint. When Colonel Wilson, furious, reprimanded him sternly, the boy looked up in amazement and said quite coolly: 'Don't make such a fuss; I haven't finished him yet!'

Master and dog were devoted, and when Colonel Wilson died, Sam lifted the coffin and slept underneath it. He was inconsolable after his master's death and was painlessly put to sleep. Thus Laugharne went on minding its own business again without fear of Sam, the St Bernard without any brandy.

A certain Danny Raye, in Dylan's Laugharne, was a local character who had once donned the uniform of a British soldier and gone to war. Henceforth the military swing of marching songs was ever in his blood. He could not resist military music and would walk at the head of the procession of the Laugharne carnival, held annually in the summer, eyes front and arms swinging as erect and serious as a Sergeant Major.

He lived in a tiny cottage on the Grist, with his wife Nell and ten children. The mantelpiece was adorned with shell-cases of various sizes on which Danny played 'The Bells of Saint Mary's' with a fork. The cottage is now empty and condemned.

When Danny's wife died, and his family left home, he lived alone in the little cottage, until the day Tommy James smelt burning, and discovered smoke pouring through the windows and door of Danny's house. He went inside and discovered Danny lying stretched out on the floor. Dragging him into the street, Tommy revived him by means of artificial respiration. When Danny came round, he asked, 'What am I doing out here in the cold? Let's go in the house for a warm.' Danny no longer lives in Laugharne, but is cared for in an old people's home in Carmarthen.

After a number of pints which he usually drank at the Fountain Inn, sometimes in Dylan's company, Danny would click his heels, and say with confidence and a wink:

'Watch Danny walk a straight line.' To prove his point, he would march across the room, as confidently as a regular on a route march.

Cockle Pickers at Ferryside

Possibly Sam of Glan-y-more

Pencil Sketch of a Donkey

Portrait of Mr Carl Eynon

Mrs Freda Ray, Danny's daughter-in-law, told me recently of Danny's latest escapade.

'The day he fetches his pension he usually goes on a drinking spree,' she said. 'There was an S.O.S. at the home when Danny failed to return one night. He was eventually found at Carmarthen hospital, his head mended with stitches. Having drunk a quantity of strong Welsh beer, he had fallen and cut his head badly.'

But the head was soon mended and Danny was none the worse for his misadventure.

Another local character is Percy John, affectionately known as Percy Ship, because he proudly served in the Royal Navy as a regular. Born and bred in Laugharne, Percy still retains the local dialect which adds charm to his conversations.

When Miss Annie of the Farmers' Arms, asked questions about local happenings, Percy would promptly reply: 'Casting thy nets again are thee?'

When Miss Annie had her feet attended to free at the clinic, because she is an old age pensioner, Percy's remark was: 'Anything for nothing and Annie's there!'

Annoyed, Miss Annie replied, 'I'd rather not tend him; see; he upsets the whole bar. I must go and get change.'

She hurries upstairs and Percy Ship winks and says: 'Annie's in the money! Bank tomorrow, she's got all her money hidden in an old stocking upstairs.'

When Miss Annie returns breathless to the bar with change she replies: 'What did you want to come here for tonight. Percy? Why didn't you stay down street?'

Percy, staring at her without a blink, says: 'I drank 'em dry, that's why I come to see thee!'

The conversation which sounds like a quarrel to a stranger, is merely good humour and no more is thought about it, but the locals enjoy it immensely.

The humorous, numerous bachelors, all over forty, who were regulars at the Farmers', were affectionately known as the 'Boys' by Miss Annie, and they were part and parcel of a happy, if unrelated, family.

All willingly ran errands for Miss Annie and her tom-cat Oliver who spent most of his life on the tiles, fathering many kittens, and was a joke amongst the 'Boys'.

Miss Annie had no slate, but wrote the debts on the beer barrels in white chalk. Sometimes when the brewery called to change the barrels, the debts were taken away too, to the relief of debtors!

Dylan also frequented the public houses of St Clears, and when he was hungry as well as thirsty, liked to call at the Butchers' Arms which is situated in the main street of Lower St Clears.

Mr Carl Eynon was not only the publican but a butcher as well, and his tiny butcher's shop was situated only a few doors away from the pub door. The small bar with the low beams and settles, and stuffed birds in glass cases, was warm and cosy, and there was often the tantalising smell of faggots or cowl wafting from the kitchen. Dylan would enquire whether Mrs Eynon was in good health, hoping that she would call him into the kitchen, which she usually did, so that he could sample some of her appetising dishes.

'He was a quiet likable man,' said Mr Eynon, 'who never caused any trouble. He told us he was writing a play for voices, adding with a smile, "I shall put you in it."'

Mr Beynon the butcher in *Under Milk Wood*, sounds very like Mr Eynon the butcher of Lower St Clears.

In his story, 'A Visit to Grandpa', Dylan writes of the visit he and his grandfather made to Llanstephan village.

The village nestles at the foot of a hill guarded by a Norman castle, which is now being restored by the Ministry of Works. Llanstephan Castle commands the grandest site in Wales. It was built to guard the entrance from the sea into the Vale of Towy, to guard Carmarthen and Dinyfawr. Together with Laugharne and Kidwelly Castles, it commanded the Carmarthenshire coast. There are no authentic records of the castle's origin. It might have been a British or perhaps a Roman camp, but the castle itself is definitely of Norman design.

In 1214, Llewelyn the Great of North Wales, demolished Llanstephan Castle and then proceeded to destroy St Clears. One writer says: 'To prevent its being turned against the peace of the county they dismantled the walls, threw down the gates, filled up the ditches and left its towers for a "habitation of owls".' However, that was not the end of Llanstephan Castle, for it was regained by the Normans and afterwards rebuilt. When Llewelyn ap Iorwerth gained victory over the English at Dinefawr in 1257, he advanced to Llanstephan, besieged the castle and took it.

Llanstephan, like Laugharne, is famous for cockle gathering, but the cockle-beds change as continually as the river changes its course. Llanstephan has vast stretches of yellow sand, and once had a beautiful wood below the castle where trees grew to enormous height and were as straight as flag-poles. The wood was called The Sticks, a misinterpretation of a local crier who mistook the Welsh word 'coed', which means wood, for sticks. The nickname clung, though Llanstephan, once famous for the 'sticks,' no longer enjoys its glory.

Once a year when visitors, usually from the Rhondda, stay in the village during the summer, there is an election of a mock-mayor in The Sticks, preceded by a carnival.

Witty and amusing speeches are made as to the merits of the prospective mayors. One character who played a big part in this entertainment was a certain Bonny who sold newspapers in Carmarthen for many years. Although he was rarely made mock-mayor, but usually the deputy mock-mayor, Bonny, a simple old man in ragged clothes, never failed to appear in Llanstephan at the appointed time.

His favourite trick to earn a pint was to recite 'The Wreck of the Hesperus' and then lie flat on the floor while customers threw water over him. He greatly appreciated the dregs of beer landlords gave him freely. Bonny died years ago, but the ceremony is still held, although The Sticks is no longer the lovely setting for the scene. The 'Village Innocent' which Dylan refers to is obviously Bonny.

Not to be outdone by the loss of Bonny, a new and lively character has taken his place called Des Cridland, a cattle drover, and a friendly familiar and amusing figure at St Clears and Carmarthen markets.

Des Cridland is, like Bonny, a 'Village Innocent' who on the day of the carnival dresses in a top hat and tails and arrives at Llanstephan believing that he will be made mayor.

Once he was elected mock-mayor and sent telegrams of good wishes to Llanstephan couples who married, signed 'Mayor of Llanstephan'. He sent a greetings telegram to Princess Alexandra and Mr Angus Ogilvy, when they married, signed the 'Mayor of Llanstephan', and had a Royal acknowledgement.

*　　*　　*　　*

70

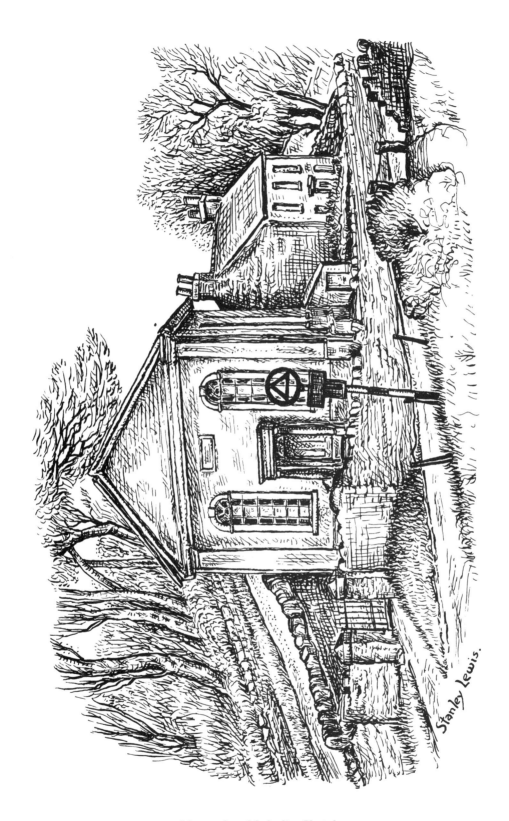

Llanstephan Methodist Chapel

A 1958 Programme of Under Milk Wood presented in The Dragon Theatre, Laugharne

A few miles from Llanstephan, in the centre of Llanybri village, stands the Marbell Church, a most unusual structure which is referred to in the Inventory of Church Goods in Edward VI's reign in 1552. It was probably built in 1388 and dedicated to the Virgin Mary. Towards the end of the nineteenth century it changed to the Congregational denomination and services were held there regularly.

During the past fifteen years it has deteriorated greatly and is now scheduled for demolition. This is sad because Llanybri lacks any other architectural interest. It is a typical white-washed Welsh village where the main language is Welsh. Cows walk aimlessly through the main street and life goes on at an unhurried pace, untypical of this century.

Keidrhych Rhys, friend of Dylan and formerly editor of the magazine *Wales*, lived there for a time with his wife, Lynette. They were married in Llanstephan Church and Dylan was the best man. Their cottage was primitive, having no water or electricity, but they brought up two fine children there.

Keidrhych, who stayed with a Mrs James and her husband, a chapel deacon, in their house at Llanstephan, the night before he married, was joined there by Dylan and Caitlin, who wanted to stay the night in the same house, but there was no room. Next day, Lynette, who had stayed at the Cottage Hotel, collected wild flowers from the banks for her wedding bouquet. After the ceremony, the bride and bridegroom with Dylan and Caitlin enjoyed a wedding breakfast of sandwiches and beer at the Castle, a public house in Llanstephan Square.

The Carmarthenshire Community Council presented *Under Milk Wood* by the Llaregyb Players for the first time on August 12th, 1958. The play was produced by Gwynne D. Evans, headmaster of a Carmarthenshire school, and Keidrhych Rhys wrote in the prologue note to the programme:

It is always a privilege to have known a writer of genius. And I knew Dylan fairly intimately for the best part of twenty years. From the time he first came to live in a two-roomed cottage in Gosport Street, Laugharne, in 1938, I visited him frequently in his various homes.

Particularly do I remember his moving respectably up the social scale to that tall lean house, Sea View, which then had a hearse parked alongside. The world seemed sunnier and more full of fun those days before the war.

Augustus John would call on Richard Hughes at the Castle; Charles Morgan wrote novels at his sister-in-law's house on Cliff Walk; Dylan was working on his collection of short stories, *Portrait of the Artist as a Young Dog*, living on various retainers and being rather absorbed by double-action yarns (which he read avidly), Chekhov and the other Russian masters.

I published his early poems, stories arid the original draft of *Quite Early One Morning* (out of which Under Milk Wood developed) in my international magazine *Wales* which for ten years was issued from various addresses in this county.

Dylan used to come and see me at Llangadog (we collaborated on one or two ill-fated ventures) and at Llanybri and the two offices of *Wales* at Carmarthen. Ebbie of Brown's Hotel and his brother Billy drove us all over the county to the Black Mountains. Llyn -v-Fan from Llandovery to Pendine.

His roots are deep in this large, neglected and lovely county. Dylan Marlais Thomas, as his second name testifies, sprang from a farming family living near that tributary river, the Marlais, above Llanwrda. That brilliant patriot, author and historian, Llewellyn Williams, also came from the same area. Dylan's grandfather, the Unitarian minister and mystic poet, Gwilym Marlais, also took the name of this stream. Abermarlais, of course, was the home of Sir Rhys ap Thomas.

Both as a Carmarthenshire man born and bred and as an early propagandist for the establishment of a Carmarthenshire Community Council, I am especially delighted that this 'play for voices' is being now produced at Dragon Park, Laugharne, as the county's main contribution to the Festival of Wales. For it is fitting that Carmarthen, as well as Edinburgh, honours Dylan.

So now Gwynne D. Evans, by staging *Under Milk Wood* with real authentic Welsh voices drawn from all over Shir Gar, gives added point to this play's imagery, universal in its impact.

In Lacharn this August week, we Carmarthen folk pay overdue homage to a son of the county whose fame is already world wide and whose poems will live forever.

On the centre pages of the programme appear the names of the cast with drawings, like this of the Mrs Dai Breads, of Polly Garter, First Narrator, Captain Cat, Second Narrator, and Eli Jenkins, the work of Stanley Lewis, who has illustrated this book.

During Laugharne's Festival Week in August 1958, Dylan's mother, who had left her flat in the Pelican, in King Street, to live in. the Boat House, wrote in a brochure:

A Message from Dylan's Mother

It gives me very great pleasure to welcome to Laugharne in this Festival Year, so many lovers of my son's work.

Although I'm unable, through ill-health, to be present at all functions in connection with this presentation of *Under Milk Wood,* I send my blessings to all those responsible for this wonderful tribute to Dylan.

Florence H. Thomas.

At that time, I was living at Orchard House, Llanstephan, when Keidrhych Rhys and his second wife Eve came down from London to see the rehearsal of *Under Milk Wood.*

They stayed with us for the night, and next day I drove them to Laugharne. It was a misty day, as so often is the case on the sea coast, and when we arrived we looked for the Llaregyb Players at Dragon Park, but were told they were rehearsing in the Memorial Hall. On reaching the Hall, we found the Players had left rehearsals for a tea break at the Cross House Inn, so patiently we awaited their return. Later, while they rehearsed, Stanley drew the main characters while Keidrhych chatted amiably to the cast.

Afterwards we all went to the Cross House, where we joined in a typically Welsh sing-song. Some of the Players had fine voices, and there was great hwyl and hymn singing at the inn that night. Next day, Keidrhych and Eve returned to London and we looked forward to the first presentation of *Under Milk Wood* in Laugharne. No one was disappointed.

For the final performance, on the Saturday night, Laugharne was in fine spirits, with its streets decorated with flags and bunting, and cars lining Victoria Street and King Street.

It was the most impressive performance possible, of which Dylan would have been proud, for the Players being Welsh did not force the accent. Finally, when the curtains were drawn, and Gwynne Evans thanked the cast for performing and the audience for coming, we felt the presence of Dylan as we sang 'Land of my fathers'.

When the audience had left, we joined Gwynne and the Players at the Cross House,

74

Carmarthen Carnival & Shopping Week

25th August—1st September, 1951

Programme 1/-   Nº 1128

Carmarthenshire Community Council

1964-65

SIXTEENTH ANNUAL REPORT

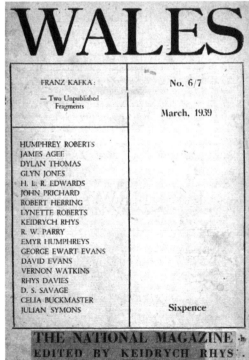

WALES

FRANZ KAFKA:	No. 6/7
— Two Unpublished Fragments	
	March, 1939
HUMPHREY ROBERTS	
JAMES AGEE	
DYLAN THOMAS	
GLYN JONES	
H. L. R. EDWARDS	
JOHN PRICHARD	
ROBERT HERRING	
LYNETTE ROBERTS	
KEIDRYCH RHYS	
R. W. PARRY	
EMYR HUMPHREYS	
GEORGE EWART EVANS	
DAVID EVANS	
VERNON WATKINS	
RHYS DAVIES	
D. S. SAVAGE	
CELIA BUCKMASTER	
JULIAN SYMONS	Sixpence

THE NATIONAL MAGAZINE
EDITED BY KEIDRYCH RHYS

CARMARTHEN SCHOOL OF ART

CENTENARY YEAR

1854

PROSPECTUS   CHURCH LANE
1953—1954   Tel. : Carmarthen 249

Collection of interesting magazine covers

Sketch of Dylan's Walk, Laugharne

Passengers in a train from Carmarthen to Swansea in 1950

where it was unanimously agreed that we should celebrate in true Welsh fashion by having a party in the marquee after 'stop tap'.

But, as we were preparing for the party, word reached us that as the curtain fell on the last performance of Dylan's *Under Milk Wood,* his mother passed peacefully away. Gloom dampened our hilarious spirits, and there was no more thought of the party that night.

During Laugharne Festival Week, the Cliff Walk, as it had always been known, was changed to Dylan's Walk and signposts were erected, one by Dylan's shed and the other by the gate of the Boat House. They were torn down by hooligans and never replaced and many people still refuse to call the walk anything but Cliff Walk.

Three years later, in 1961, the Llaregyb Players returned again. By this time we were living at Upton House, Laugharne, a tall Georgian house opposite the Memorial Hall. I had taken to Laugharne and the people as a duck takes to water, having known many of them for years, and I found them tolerant, kind, and full of understanding; their language was English, and Billy Williams, then portreeve, made us feel at home. When preparations were made for the second festival of Laugharne I felt as if I had never lived anywhere else.

The locals were not over-enthusiastic that *Milk Wood* should be performed again in Laugharne, but they accepted the plan with resignation.

Dragon Park was not available this time, and three alternatives remained. A marquee within the Castle walls would be picturesque and ideal, except for the fear of falling masonry. The Cors field, which is a marshy piece of land, was also rejected and the choice fell on Wooford Field, which is the highest part of Laugharne and faces the blast of the strong south-westerly gales that blow so strongly from the sea.

This time, Jim Jones, who had been the First Narrator in the Llaregyb Players' first production, wrote the tribute to Dylan Thomas.

He came early to his long home
Without feeling the grasshopper's burden
Nor seeing the mourners going about in the streets.
A rare child paddling in the tributaries of the morning
Until Death took his hand like a finicky father and dragged him home. The call
    was so sudden that we did not see his smile of farewell, nothing but dust
    returning to dust as a cell door shuts overnight.
We shall not see again the humour in the drunken clothes,
Nor feel his voice creating word after word like the sound of a sea lurching on the
    rocks.
A clean cross sprouts on the aftermath of bones
And nothing remains but the harsh kiss of memories.
We remember his song of mischief in
    teasing the Hunchback in the kennel in the Park or
    cursing God for watching the sparrows fall.
I tarry in this cemetary of hiraeth
Not because he knew and loved his mother-tongue
Nor because he sang a selfless psalm in Salem.
He sought his bible in an English pub in English Laugharne
Playing a waiting game with words and gods

I tarry in this cemetary of hiraeth since his soul drifts for ever above the tombs as
    new and fresh as the birth of a baby in an old bed.
And through the dusty windows of the earth
He hears the lament of Laugharne.
The gossips from the Llaregybs of the World,
And from the threshold of Bethesda,
A song and a prayer,

Our father which art in heaven
Lead us not into temptation,
But into that Presence and Peace,
Where death shall have no dominion.

Laugharne was again full of strangers, they came from everywhere to pay tribute, the locals watched, listened but said little. The week commenced with the annual carnival and dance, then the band of the Royal Welch Fusiliers with Taffy, their goat mascot, marched up and down the Grist playing martial music.

Stanley Lewis held an exhibition of paintings in Laugharne Schoolroom, and Anne and Allan Lloyd a pottery exhibition. Inquisitive reporters prowled everywhere.

One night, gale force winds ripped the marquee and, although the Players and the members of Laugharne Athletic Club worked on it all day, one show could not go on. But next day, the marquee was repaired and *Under Milk Wood* went on as if nothing unusual had happened.

Again it was a successful week, and when it was over the B.B.C. visited Laugharne, to find out what the people of Laugharne felt about the fame of Dylan Thomas, for strangers were surprised that Laugharne had not commercialised Dylan, surprised at their indifference towards him. Many people were interviewed by Kenneth Allsop of the 'Tonight' programme and gave their varying views. Some felt strongly that Dylan had ridiculed them in *Under Milk Wood,* others wondered why so much fuss was made of a man who, to them, had looked and behaved no different from a workman. There was very little hero-worship in Laugharne.

He had been one of them, no more, no less, and they wondered what all the talk was about!

The third festival was held from July 29th, 1964, to August 1st, 1964, and this time the marquee theatre was erected at Glanymor in a field overlooking the estuary above the Boat House.

The week again began with the Saturday carnival, community singing on the Sunday night, and the Welch Fusilier band marched through Laugharne playing military music on the Monday night.

An exhibition was held at Laugharne school by the staff of Carmarthen School of Art, and pupils from Laugharne, Pendine and Llanelly schools competed for prizes in shell arrangement, embroidery and painting, there was also a flower and cake show. As I watched visitors walking about, Dick Lewis, the milk, smiled and said to me in his quiet cultivated voice: 'Dylan would be amused to see these people coming to Laugharne to see *Under Milk Wood,* I can see him now in his baggy trousers, tweed jacket and tousled hair walking down Victoria Street carrying a string-bag. Why, they would look at Dylan and wonder who the strange untidy little man could be.'

When I saw the last performance of *Under Milk Wood* on Saturday, August 1st, 1964, I looked around the marquee and saw only six Laugharne people, the rest were strangers.

At the end of yet another splendid performance, the Portreeve of Laugharne, Ralph Tucker, who incidentally played one of Mrs Pritchard's late husbands in the play, appealed for funds to build a permanent memorial theatre in Laugharne.

After the hard work involved in erecting a marquee a permanent theatre would be a blessing, but Laugharne people are not enthusiastic, except perhaps the business people who have everything to gain.

'We like it quiet,' the old people say, and that perhaps is what Dylan admired most of all when he wrote: 'They envy Laugharne its minding of its own, strange, business; its sane disregard for haste.'

The American writer John Brinnin seemed surprised when he wrote:

Dylan's greetings to the villagers and theirs to him were mad in mumblings and monosyllables, a sort of respectful, familiar, yet at the same time distant exchange. They knew, of course, that he had business in the big world, that he had been to America, and that he was regarded importantly in London, and most of them had probably heard him on the wireless or seen him on television. Yet nothing in their manner toward him suggested that they were particularly impressed, or even that they understood just what Dylan's distinction was. For his part and without effort, Dylan's manner in his own village seemed, to be directed toward looking and acting as much like everyone else as possible.

Viola Potgieter, an American lady from Rockford, Illinois, came with her husband Fred to Laugharne because she admired Dylan's poetry, and wanted to see the places that Dylan wrote about. When I wrote and told her of my plans for writing the story of Laugharne and Dylan, she replied:

I feel you could do a fine thing with Dylan if you keep to the intimate and pleasant details before his coming to America. Fame is a hideous experience to many people. People go crazy over celebrities and ruin them by attention. I believe you could write a good foil for these self-appointed seers who treat Dylan like a mystic.

He was a painter of big canvases throwing the words as an artist might dash on blobs of paint. But one loses the picture when one gets snagged on a few startling words and phrases.

*   *   *   *

Another big festival time in Carmarthenshire is New Year's Eve and New Year's Day. Christmas Eve is celebrated with festive spirit, but New Year's Eve is the more important of the two.

In Welsh Wales, it is known as 'Dydd Calan'. In most Carmarthen villages and towns, schoolchildren go to every house on New Year's Day, wishing the occupants a Happy New Year in return for a penny or two. On New Year's Eve, it is still the custom for the farmers and villagers to go round farms and houses wishing each other a Happy New Year after twelve o'clock-'Blwyddyh Newydd dda'.

The well-wishers usually have a few drinks at each farmhouse after singing a carol or two. Sometimes the celebrations continue throughout the night, and there are many aching heads on New Year's Day.

For the comfortable stay-at-homes, there is very little sleep on New Year's Eve, for no sooner has one group wished you a Happy New Year with renderings of 'Come All Ye Faithful', than another group arrive with well wishes.

I remember such a night when I joined some carollers to wish a neighbouring farmer a 'Happy New Year'. The weary farmer and his family were in bed, and refused to open house for us, but threw money out instead. The money rolled away and was lost in the darkness.

In his excitement to find it, one of our group tripped and fell against the cowshed door, our singing was then enriched by the plaintive mooing of six or seven cows. I believe we sang Cwm Rhondda and Cara Lan on that occasion.

No doubt Dylan went on one of these escapades and knew the fun and laughter it involved.

Mary Curtis wrote of celebrations of an earlier century:

On New Year's Day, the boys of the town paid an early visit to the bedroom of the master and mistress of the different houses, carrying branches of rosemary dipped in water, with which they sprinkled their faces, wishing a Happy New Year. They would carry pieces of the box-tree and cups of water, sprinkling everyone they met.

In 1873, it was discontinued for the first time and I have not heard of it since; but in Pendine the children do still, on Old New Year's Day, which occurs on the 12th of January, come early to the houses and sprinkle about the passages with branches of box while they repeat an ancient piece of poetry.

Some of the best families would say to those they liked and respected, 'Bring us New Year's Water'. There was a feeling at this time that it was fortunate or unfortunate if the name of the first person they saw on New Years morning began with a fortunate or unfortunate letter. H, J and R were fortunate, for they denoted Happiness or Health joy and Riches. The letters T, W and S foretold Trouble, Worry and Sorrow. The anxiety was to be the first to wish a Happy New Year. They would go to the door of some house and knock as the clock struck twelve midnight. The inmates asked the name of the person who knocked. If it began with an unlucky letter, they did not open the door, nor if it were a woman, since it was considered unfortunate to see a woman the first of the year. The young boys who were to be apprenticed to a trade gathered money on this day from the different houses to help them in their start in life.

Originally this custom was confined to those who were to be masons or carpenters. They carried square boxes, with a slot in the middle for money, ornamented with crosses and hearts, with the words: 'The Apprentices of Laugharne', inscribed.

A verse sung in Wales on New Year's Day, runs:

> Here we bring fresh water
> From the well so clear
> For to worship God with
> This happy New Year.
> Sing Levy dew, sing Levy dew,

Portrait of Miss Curtis

Horsepool Road, Laugharne

The water and the wine
With the seven golden wives,
And the bugles that do shine.
Sing rains a fair maid,
With gold upon her toe;
Open you the West door,
And let the Old Year go,
Sing Rains, a fair maid,
With gold upon her chin;
Open you the East door,
And let the New Year in.

Rosie Probert (softly):
What seas did you see,
Tom Cat, Tom Cat,
In your sailoring days
Long long ago?
What sea beasts were
In the wavery green
When you were my master?

This is the authentic story of a woman called Rosie Probert who lived in a small cottage in Horsepool Road, Laugharne. Dylan had never met her, but her name seemed to fascinate him and he probably heard the story from the locals of the child staying with Rosie Probert who had run from the cottage to the bridge over the stream at the bottom of Horsepool Road to see the ducks that swam there. She leaned too far over the bridge parapet, lost her balance, fell into the stream and was drowned.

Captain Cat:
I'll tell you the truth.
Seas barking like seals,
Blue seas and green,
Seas covered with eels
And mermen and whales.

Captain Cat the dreamer, recalling his seafaring days with yearning, because he knew they had gone for ever. How many tales of the sea had Dylan heard from Johnny Thomas (Holloway), who lived at Myrtle Cottage, a house built under the bank near Holloway Field? Johnny Holloway, as he was called locally, was proud of his connections with the sea, as his father and grandfather had been before him. Their small schooner, *Nautilus*, sailed to Bideford in Devon for bricks, and to Kidwelly in Carmarthenshire for coal. (Dylan called Captain Cat's cruiser the S.S. *Kidwelly*.) They anchored the *Nautilus* at the Pill, which is underneath the high banks of the castle. Horses and carts were driven there to unload the coal, later to be distributed amongst the people.

Johnny Thomas, Holloway, was born on the Strand, at the house called Lorenzo, which is divided from the sea by a solidly built high wall.

He often retold the story of the rough windy day when a local man was warned by more experienced boatmen, not to risk going out in his rowing boat. Ignoring their advice, the foolish man went out to sea. That night, Johnny's sister Polly walked to the end of the wall to look out to sea for signs of her father's schooner returning from Kidwelly, but instead of seeing the schooner, she saw a light appear below the wall, followed by four men carrying a ladder with a man's body on it. Frightened at the sight, she ran into the house to relate what she had seen.

Enquiries were made locally, and it was ascertained that no one was dead, and no one had walked under the wall carrying a ladder that night. However, next day, the apparition that Polly had seen so plainly came to life, when the body of the man who had neglected the rough weather warning, was found drowned. His body was carried past the wall on a ladder just as she had seen it the night before. The belief of the light before death, was obviously prevalent in Laugharne then.

Johnny Thomas went to school at Minerva, a tall grey house in King Street, where he paid one penny a week for his education.

When Johnny was old enough to work, he went to sea with his father, and they often stayed in a flea-ridden lodging house in Saundersfoot. In those days most Welshmen wore under their trousers long Welsh flannel drawers tied around their ankles with tapes. Old Johnny would untie the tapes of his flannel drawers to catch the numerous fleas that harboured there after a night spent at the lodging house.

Johnny would take any medicine prescribed if he thought he would be cured.

At one time he suffered from asthma and was prescribed a cure by a local quack. 'Boil a quantity of snails and drink the broth,' he was told. Without hesitation, Johnny took the advice, drank the water in which he had boiled the snails and, according to him, was cured of asthma for ever.

When he was an old man, Johnny remained a tough character who thought nothing of climbing an apple tree to reach the best apples, which always grew at the top; he was in his eighties at the time and was continually warned that he might fall, but he would sit on the top branch smoking his pipe and enjoying the scenery. The smoke ascending from the top of the tree looked for all the world as if the tree was on fire.

He grew his own tobacco and dried the leaves on rope-lines in the kitchen. When the leaves were dry enough, he sorted them out carefully and poured on them the best navy rum, then he rolled the leaves into a kind of large cigar, covering the mixture with stockingette, and binding it with twine, until it resembled a mummy.

The maturing tobacco had a fragrant smell, and when it was mature Johnny sliced it like a cake. The smell when he smoked it was rather overpowering and choking.

Sometimes, when he had no tobacco, Johnny smoked the dried leaves of the Colts-foot herb, a weed that has almost covered the graves in the old churchyard of Laugharne.

Johnny Holloway was a drinking friend of Dylan. Every morning as regular as clockwork, he would leave his cottage to walk to the Cross House for a pint or two, on passing the doors of his neighbours he never failed to call out cheerfully, "Ow are yer today?'

It was his proud boast that he had drunk enough beer to float a ship, and according to his niece who looked after him in his old age, he was a real gossip, knowing all the local news from down-street to up-street. Doubtless Dylan listened to his tales and was amused by local stories, for were they not pub companions?

When Johnny was eighty-seven, he broke a leg and was admitted to Carmarthen hospital where he overheard a nurse telling the doctor that lie would never recover. Then wisely he thought to himself 'I will recover, and I will walk again', and he did!

Corner Shop in the Grist, Laugharne

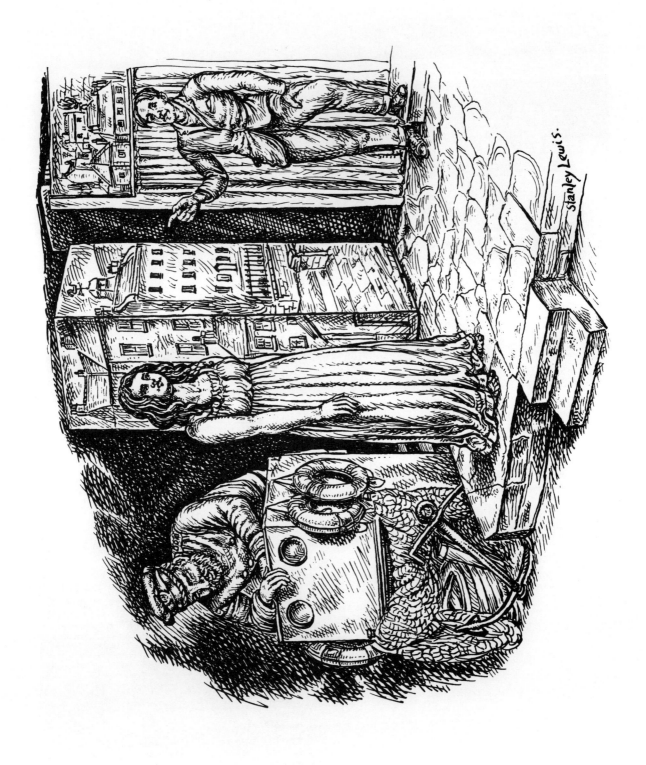

Narrator, Rosie Probert, Captain Cat

Being of a strong sea-faring constitution, he was not often ill, but one cold damp winter he was confined to bed. The doctor called on him and said sharply, 'You are to stop in bed until I call again.'

A year later, Johnny spoke to Mr Thomas the chemist.

'Will you ask the doctor when I can get up, Mr Thomas, and will you ask him when he is going to call?' he chuckled.

The chemist gave the doctor the message, whereupon the doctor replied, 'Don't say the old so and so is still in bed?' Needless to say, Johnny had only stayed in bed a day.

Other times when the doctor called on him, Johnny would extend his hand and say, 'Feel my pulse, Doctor, 'ow is it now?' 'Like an ox,' the doctor would reply, and Johnny was satisfied that he was well and very much alive.

He became the oldest shareholder (burgess) in Laugharne, and died when he was eighty-nine, his last request being for water from the Lakes, and some good strong beer.

Once a year, he went to Plashett Chapel anniversary service and proudly placed a pound note on the plate, and he gave his niece five shillings a year to clean the family graves.

Towards the end of his life he became blind, but after an eye operation he could see well enough to walk about. Was he perhaps the character on whom Dylan based Captain Cat? Johnny Thomas, Holloway, died in Laugharne, but the schooner *Nautilus* sank off the Mumbles.

> What big seas of dreams ran in the Captain's sleep?
> Over what blue-whaled waves did he sail through a rainbow hail of
> flying-fishes to the music of Circe's swinish island?
> Do not let him be dreaming of dividends and bottled beer and onions.

Johnny was a firm believer in salts for health, and so was Dylan, as a local woman once observed when she was shopping in a small grocery shop. Caitlin had sent a girl to the shop with her grocery list, on the back of the list was a poem written by Dylan. The woman clearly remembers the gist of the poem because she thought it amusing.

Dylan discovered his stomach was not working properly, for his mind was muddled and he could not think clearly. He realised it was time to take 'opening medicine', so he took a glass of water, stirred in a quantity of salts, and watched the crystals slowly dissolving until the smell reached his nostrils and almost made him sick.

After a lot of thought, he plucked up sufficient courage to swallow the medicine in one gulp, discovering as he did so that the taste was not as bad as he anticipated; nevertheless he took a drink of something stronger to take the taste away. Satisfied at last, that his health would obviously improve, he was working quietly when there was an ominous rumble. He left his work and ran. The last word on the paper was 'nothingness!'

Below the Boathouse stands the Ferry House, once an inn where the locals were reported to flock on Sundays because it was out of the way.

A family called Roberts lived there, whose livelihood was running the ferry boat between Laugharne and Llanstephan, fishing for dabs and sewin, and shooting teal, wild duck and rabbits. Jack the Ferry as he was then called, was the eldest of the family and he often had the job of fetching the girls across from Llanstephan to meet their boy friends in Laugharne. Once he took advantage of the situation; a fight ensued and Jack had his eye kicked out by an irate boy friend.

Dai and Na Roberts hawked the fish they caught about Laugharne in large panniers strapped across their shoulders, Dai was particularly amusing, for he had the habit of tapping at the door of a house and asking the housewife, 'Any fish today Mrs so and so?' If the woman replied 'No,' Dai, feeling hurt, would say 'All right, Annie,' or whatever Christian name she had. If she replied, 'Yes,' Dai would say, smiling, 'All right, Mrs So and so.' Na Roberts died of tetanus when a fork went into his foot.

A sister called Mary Anne was a cripple. When she was expecting a child, the man responsible denied being the father. Mary Anne said to him. 'If the child is a deaf mute, you will know it is yours.' Apparently deaf mutes were common in his family. A male child was born to Mary Anne, and he was a deaf mute, but the father did not marry her. The child became known as Budha, and was later to become the man of whom mention has already been made, suspected but acquitted of murdering Lizzie Thomas, the aged spinster in her tiny cottage in Clifton Street.

Being a cripple, Mary Anne was unable to walk around much, but she ran the house efficiently from her armchair, with orders given as clearly as by a sergeant major. Her voice rang like a bell through the house,

'Clean the potatoes, Dai.'

'Right!'

'Put them on to boil.'

'Right.'

'Add salt.'

'Right!'

'Turn the birds now.' (They usually had a bird apiece, maybe a wild pigeon or a wild duck.)

'Right!'

'Wash the slugs out of the cabbage. '

'Right!'

'Put a saucepan of clean water on to boil.'

'Right!'

So her orders continued until the dinner was cooked and the household chores completed.

Dai, Na and Jack collected the groceries from the shop in a sack. They have been dead for many years now, but the memory of them will linger long in Laugharne, for they were among the colourful characters that gave Laugharne its charm.

'Who impressed you most in America?' Dylan was asked. He replied without hesitation, 'Charlie Chaplin, the clown and the greatest actor of the silent screen.'

Dylan lived his life among the clowns of Laugharne. Dylan, Howard Dark, Billy Williams and Dai Thomas when having a peaceful drink together were joined by a man only known by Howard Dark. Without hesitating, Howard Dark introduced the man to his drinking friends.

'This is Mr Billy Williams of the Pioneer Buses,' he said, 'And this is Mr Dylan Thomas, the well known poet,' then, pointing to Dai Thomas, he said, 'This is Mr Dai Thomas.'

'Aye,' replied Dai smiling, 'Dai Thomas, small coal.'

The name stuck and he has been called Dai Small Coal ever since! Needless to say he is quite proud of it. When Dylan's parents lived in the ground floor flat at the Pelican, Dai Thomas and his family lived in the upstairs flat, so he has a wide knowledge of the Thomas

Passengers in Pioneer Bus, Laugharne

Interior of Town Hall, Laugharne

family. He remembers that Mrs Florence Thomas did not like to be told that Dylan inherited his brains from his father, a Grammar School master of English at Swansea.

Dylan rarely wore socks during the summer months but walked about in a pair of plimsoles. When he was asked by a local whether he was going to change to meet a friend who was visiting him in Laugharne, he replied, 'I have changed, I've put my socks on!'

Miss Annie Jeremy told me of a wedding she remembers as a child, it stands out clearly in her memory because it was so different from most weddings.

The bride was Maggie Butler, a middle-aged lady living in Laugharne; her wedding dress was an ordinary dress, a shawl, an apron and a lace cap, her bridegroom was an Irish tinker called Simon. Mr Attenbury, the curate, married them, and there were only two other people in church.

Turning to Maggie Butler, the curate said in a low distant voice, 'Repeat this after me.'

The bride blushing a little and swaying awkwardly on her feet replied, 'Oh dear, I can't say it, but I'll 'ave 'im.'

'But you must say it,' insisted the curate.

Simon the tinker found the service difficult too, and when he came to a different portion to repeat, he said unabashed, 'Oh that's rather 'ard, I'll think I'll skip that.'

The curate was firm and determined that the service should be performed properly. 'You'll skip nothing,' he insisted, and the bride and bridegroom were forced to remain until they were properly married. There was no confetti, cameras or wedding breakfast, but the bride was as happy as a lark when she left the church on the arm of her tinker bridegroom. They returned to live at the Lakes, where Simon had a tinker's shop.

Once a flea man lodged in Horsepool Road. He trained fleas to perform and pull small carts, and they performed in a show on the Grist. At that time the locals humorously re-christened Horsepool Road Flea Street; it has now reverted to its original name.

A local man who became obstreperous after a quantity of beer was often locked in the jail for the night. The jail, a small barred room under the Town Hall, was an easy access for the locals, who continued to feed the man beer through a teapot spout. The man proved more drunk than ever in the courtroom next morning. There were many practical jokers in Laugharne in those days. People made their own fun, for there was no entertainment apart from local fairs that arrived in certain months of the year.

Not so many years ago, groups of miners from the Rhondda sailed to Laugharne on fishing sprees, congregating on the Grist square for a typical Welsh hymn song. Many of the local people, unable to find jobs in Laugharne, were forced to go to the Maerdy coal-mines to work, and in those days these people encouraged the miners to come to Laugharne for a holiday.

One youth who went to Maerdy to work was Brinley Davies, who was born and bred in a tiny cottage in Gosport Street. Many years later he returned to Laugharne and sang with the miners on the Grist. Miss Gladys Jeremy heard him and noticed his voice was outstanding. She encouraged the youth to give up the mines and to have his voice trained, and she eventually succeeded in gaining him a scholarship to the Royal Academy of Music, London. Brinley Davies did not return to Laugharne after his training but was reputed to have gone abroad for a job. However, he wrote a book called Seth, taking the *nom de plume* of David Brinley; the book. has a strong Laugharne flavour.

Dylan wrote in *Quite Early One Morning:* 'I walked on to the cliff path again, the town behind and below waking up now so very slowly; I stopped and turned and looked.'

There is no walk more exhilarating than the cliff path in the early morning. The bay becoming alive with bird life and the first expectant sounds of daybreak. Dylan wrote: 'Someone has been dreaming of reading Charles Morgan.'

Charles Morgan spent much time in Laugharne, at the home of his sister-in-law, Miss Elizabeth Vaughane, who lives in a house above the cliff path. He stayed in Laugharne when Dylan lived at the Boat House, and they must have met one another often while walking across the cliff to their respective homes.

From *Quite Early One Morning, Under Milk Wood* was born.

'I am Captain Tiny Evans, my ship was the Kidwelly,
And Mrs Tiny Evans has been dead for many a year;
"Poor Captain Tiny all alone" the neighbours whisper
But I like it all alone and I hated her.
Open the curtains, light the fire, what are servants for?
I am Mrs Ogmore Pritchard and I want another snooze.
Dust the china, feed the canary, sweep the dressing-room floor;
And before you let the sun in, mind he wipes his shoes.'

Thus some of the voices of a cliff-perched town at the far end of Wales moved out of sleep and darkness into the newborn ancient and ageless morning, moved and were lost.

When *Under Milk Wood* was performed for the first time in London, many of the locals were invited to see it. Billy Williams was one of the few who went.

After the performance, someone tentatively asked him: 'Well, Billy, how did you like it?'

'Good God,' Billy exclaimed, 'I thought I was back in Laugharne'

92

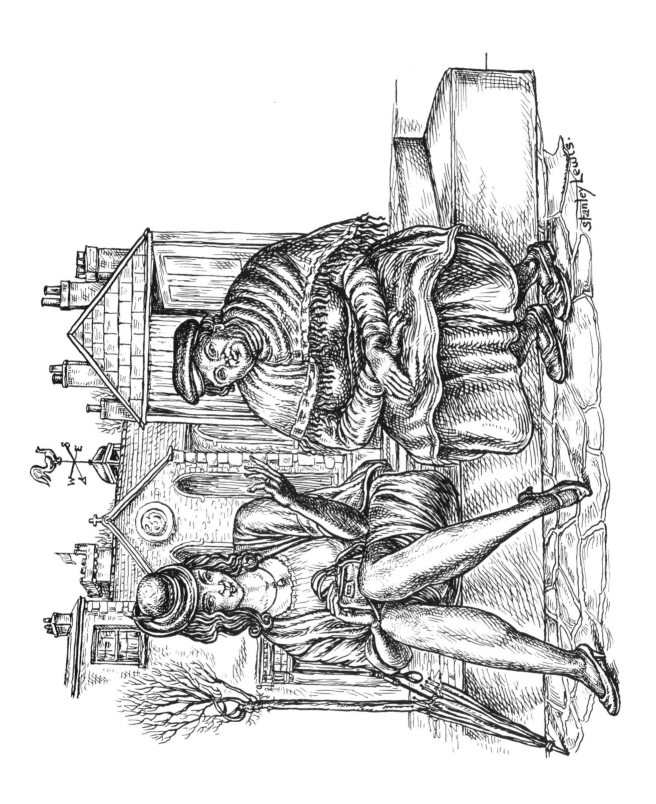

Mrs Dai Bread 1 and Mrs Dai Bread 2

Town Hall, Laugharne

DYLAN AT LAUGHARNE

When Dylan came to Laugharne in 1938, Chancellor S. B. Williams the vicar, was portreeve, and Dylan, who was a guest at the portreeve's breakfast, proposed the toast to the ladies who had worked long hours preparing and serving the food which the men had eaten.

After speeches are made by important guests, the portreeve, wearing his purple robe and chain of office, consisting of a gold and enamel pendant bearing the corporation's coat of arms hung by links of gold cockleshells. (Each portreeve adds a gold cockleshell with his name inscribed on the back.) The recorder, who holds the office for his lifetime, foreman, bailiff, jurymen, common attorneys, constables, halberdiers, mattockmen, flagbearers, guides, vicar and guests walk in procession from the Town Hall to the church for morning service.

Dylan came to Laugharne by invitation of Richard Hughes, author of *High Wind* in *Jamaica*, who had rented the Georgian house adjoining the castle from the Starke family.

Augustus John was staying at the house with Caitlin Macnamara at the time. This was fortunate for Dylan, for it was Augustus John who had first introduced him to Caitlin at the Wheatsheaf, London, and now he was to meet her again and marry her.

Dylan later wrote of Laugharne: 'And some, like myself, just came, one day, for the day, and never left; got off the bus and forgot to get on again.'

There was never any talk or suggestion, much less evidence, of Dylan having affairs with women in Laugharne or Carmarthen.

'He never bothered with women,' the locals say. 'He liked his beer and cigarettes. Perhaps he loved his wife too much.'

Billy Williams, who accompanied Dylan on many trips around the county, told me the story of the day he and Dylan went to Carmarthen together. Their first port of call was the Glue Pot, a public house, partly in Jackson's Lane and partly in King Street. The downstairs bars were overcrowded, so Billy and Dylan made their way upstairs to a roomier lounge which they discovered to be full of girls and women. Glancing around the room, Billy smiled at Dylan and jokingly asked: 'Which one will you have Dylan? Take your pick.'

Dylan grimaced, looked around the room and indicated that he had chosen a woman in the far corner.

'That one,' he replied wryly.

'But she's the ugliest woman in the room,' Billy protested.

'I know that; that is why I chose her. Not so many men will have been with her,' was Dylan's prompt reply.

The story of the trip that Brinnin, and Dylan, Caitlin, and Bill Read and Billy Williams made to St David's Cathedral in Pembrokeshire, told by John Brinnin in his book, *Dylan Thomas in America*, is slightly different from Billy Williams's version:

The day was warm and sunny when we left Laugharne. Dylan sat in the front seat next to me, Caitlin, Bill Read and John Brinnin sat in the back seat as I drove from

Laugharne to St Clears to follow the Haverfordwest road. Our first stop was at Robeston Wathen for a few drinks, which Dylan paid for. When we reached Haverfordwest we stopped and called at the Castle Hotel for drinks, Dylan paid. From Haverfordwest we drove to Newgale, then to Solva, where we stopped for drinks, Dylan paid.

When we reached St David's Cathedral, the weather had worsened to a misty drizzle, and the pubs were closed.

John Brinnin and Bill Read were impressed by the Cathedral, saying they would like to transport it to America. They took photographs and then Dylan suggested a meal, so I drove them to the Grove for tea. Again Dylan paid. I was amazed to see Bill Read swallowing quantities of pills, they were all colours and looked like liquorice comfits.

As the weather was so miserable, Caitlin wanted to go straight back to Laugharne, but Dylan wished to make the day memorable and enjoyable, and suggested having dinner in Newport, Pembrokeshire.

It was a tasty lobster dinner, costing nearly six pounds, I offered to pay my share, but the Yanks did not bat an eyelid when Dylan paid, which caused Caitlin to remark to them, 'Haven't you got any hands or pockets?'

It was a disappointing day. Mournfully, everyone climbed into the car, and Caitlin sat in front with me, while Dylan fell asleep between John Brinnin and Bill Read in the back. The drizzle had turned to heavy rain, and on the way to Crymmych, we passed a fair on the side of the road which Caitlin was anxious to attend. We stopped for another drink further on, but Dylan and John Brinnin remained in the car. The trip that had begun with so much expectation, with Dylan anxious that his guests should enjoy the day, ended with tension and despair.

Before Dylan went to America he suffered blackouts. Once he fell like a stone as he stood by the mantelpiece of the bar in Brown's Hotel. Billy Williams picked him up, and when he came round his first words were, 'How long was I out?'

'Two minutes,' replied Billy.

'Oh it wasn't long that time,' said Dylan, and ordered another drink as if nothing unusual had happened.

Most Laugharne people were angry with Brinnin's book revealing Dylan as a raving boozer and woman-mad lunatic; they do not and will not believe that the Dylan they knew acted so stupidly.

'Why did the Yanks make a fool of him?' they ask. Perhaps because he was an individualist.

After Dylan's mother died, Caitlin's visits to Laugharne grew ever more infrequent.

*   *   *   *

One particularly warm, sunny day, my husband and I with our young daughter Jennifer went to visit her at the Boat House. The door was opened by Cliff Gordon, an actor from Wales, who had played the part of the postman in the London production of *Under Milk Wood*. He invited us in, telling us that he had written a one-act play that afternoon called *The Smugglers and the Exciseman* for Dylan's three children to act in the shed at the back of the house. Inside, the children were busy making costumes. Caitlin had walked along the estuary looking for her son Llewellyn, who had gone out in the rowing-boat. Outside in the sunshine, Caitlin's sister Nicolette and brother-in-law, Anthony Devas, and Miss Geraldine Laurence from Tenby sat sunning themselves.

96

Miss Annie Jeremy, Licensee of The Farmers Arms, Laugharne

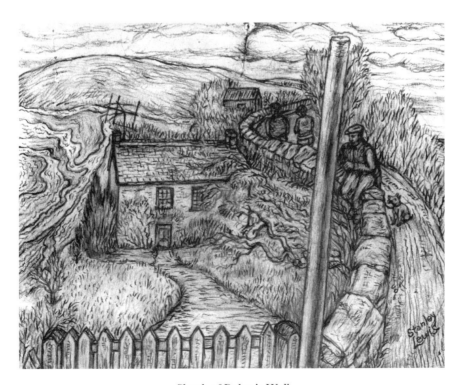

Sketch of Dylan's Walk

Portrait of Mrs Bertha Williams

Caitlin appeared in time for the play, and we all squeezed into the small shed with the ricketty boards. Backed by Cliff Gordon the children acted well, and we ended the entertainment by singing and dancing.

A few nights later we were invited to dinner at the house of Miss Geraldine Laurence at Tenby. Rollie McKenna, the American photographer, Caitlin, Llewellyn and Howard Dark went in Rollie's hired car, Cliff Gordon, Stanley and I in ours.

There were several intellectual London guests at the house, and after a few drinks and introductions in the lounge, we ate a mixed grill dinner in the basement kitchen, served on a long table covered in a gay oil-cloth. Later we returned to the lounge where we played games. Before we left, Caitlin signed her book, *Left Over Life to Kill*, for Geraldine Laurence.

A few days later, Caitlin and her children left for Italy, and she has not lived in the Boat House since, although she paid a flying visit to Laugharne a few years ago.

Now, the Boat House remains empty most of the year. It is an attractively situated house at the end of the Cliff Walk where the banks are draped with old-man's-beard in autumn, and with blackthorn bushes, virginal white, in spring. Tucked away on the edge of the sandstone rock, it stands like a lighthouse, keeping a wary eye on the incoming tides, listening to the cries of curlews, oyster catchers and screeching gulls, watching the herons fishing in the pools and the cormorants playing hide-and-seek, seeing the patchwork fields of Llanstephan and Llanybri across the bay, and patiently waiting for the poet who left full of expectations but never returned.

It is sad to see the lonely house, waiting like a prostrated mother who will never see her son again.

At the top end of the long narrow garden stands the blue-painted wooden shed where Dylan worked and wrote at a rough, scrubbed-top table. Coconut matting covers the draughty wooden floor, ivy creeps through the cracks, and the branches of a fig tree tap the window like ghostly fingers.

Pinned on the walls are prints of Pierre Bonnard's 'La Famille Terrasse,' a printed photograph of the American poet, Walt Whitman, and many prints of Peter Brueghel's work, the early Flemish painter of village life and village characters.

The shed has two windows and their pink velvet curtains are faded and cobwebbed. It is sad to see the fine mahogany bookcase standing empty, yet, though his books no longer grace it, the spirit of Dylan is surely there, searching the estuary for sea birds, and looking for the hawk hovering over Sir John's Hill.

When Dylan had his last Laugharne haircut in Victoria Street, Mrs Dark recalls that she clipped and cut his locks and then showed him the results in a large mirror.

'Does that please you?' she asked.

'Yes,' he replied. 'It will last me a lifetime.' It did.

Dylan's stature changed from a tough to a toff when he vacated his two-roomed cottage in Gosport and moved to Sea View, a four-storied house, up-street, near the castle. It would be difficult to imagine Dylan filling the many rooms with furniture he did not own, and so the house must have seemed spacious but rather hollow during his stay there. Augustus John was a frequent visitor, so what the house lacked in furniture it gained by the interesting variety of people who were continual guests.

Mrs Bertha Williams, an elderly widow, worked for Dylan and Caitlin when they lived at Sea View with Llewellyn, then their only child. She insists that Caitlin was a good mother who took endless trouble to feed her child properly; During those years, strained vegetables for babies could not be bought in tins as today, and Caitlin was always grating carrots and other vegetables for her boy.

They were a happy couple, and I never saw bottles of spirits in the house all the time I was there. There was always plenty of beer and stout, mind you. Dylan would write in the mornings and Caitlin practised dancing.

They always went for a drink before lunch. I've seen them without a penny but there was always plenty of food in the house. The tradesmen gave them credit because they knew they would be paid when Dylan's cheques came-they were very honest people. He did not have a regular wage so they lived in a simple way, no fuss, no style. When Augustus John stayed there, I lent them a few chairs, and when they went away for a short holiday, I looked after Llewellyn in my cottage.

There was no bathroom in Sea View, and because it is a tall lean house it looks bigger than it really is. They ate their meals in the kitchen and Dylan wrote on the second floor; they usually went to bed between ten and eleven o'clock at night, rising between nine and ten in the morning.

Dylan's mother and father lived at Llangain then, but they often came to Sea View for holidays.

One Sunday night, Dylan was closing the upstairs window when the sash cords snapped and the window fell on his hands. Mrs Tudor Williams could hear him calling 'Bertha! Bertha!' and hurried to tell me. I went upstairs as quickly as I could and released him.

All the time I was there, I never heard him speak about his work, but I knew he loved Laugharne. He was always giving me tips, and I can't speak too highly of him or Caitlin. They never went to church or chapel, but you can't say they were heathens, and he didn't drink more than anyone else. I can't believe he did what they say he did in America. If that is so then he wasn't the Dylan we knew in Laugharne.

Dylan, anxious that Llewellyn should be like other boys, was angry with Caitlin when she darned his grey school socks with red wool; he knew how cruel the world can be to a schoolboy.

*   *   *   *

Fern Hill Farm, where Dylan spent many happy childhood days, is quite unlike the average Welsh farmhouse. Set amidst a variety of trees with a trout stream nearby, it has an air of decaying superiority, both in architecture and legend, and seems out of place in the austere village of Llangain.

Dylan's childhood at Fern Hill was clearly recalled in 'The Peaches':

Then a door at the end of the passage opened; I saw the plates on the shelves, the lighted lamp on the long, oil-clothed table, 'Prepare to Meet thy God' knitted over the fire-place, the smiling china dogs, the brown-stained settle, the grandmother clock, and I ran into the kitchen and into Annie's arms.

The legend of the hangman who lived at Fern Hill a century ago, must have set Dylan's vivid imagination swinging, for he performed his lurid duties at Carmarthen gaol.

100

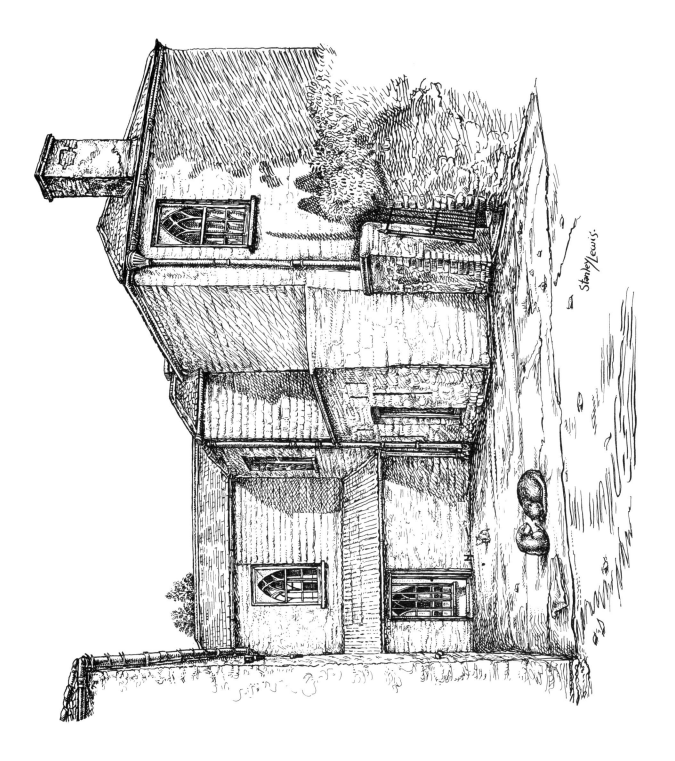

Fern Hill Farm, Laugharne

Carmarthenshire Hill Farm, Cwmllyfri,
in the County Hall Collection

A definite bit of Carmarthenshire has place in Royal Academy

Ever since 1932 Mr. Stanley Lewis, Principal of the Carmarthen School of Art, has had drawings, portraits and other oil paintings in the Royal Academy.

This year his "Welsh Dresser" is well hung in the same gallery as the Simon Elves portrait of the Queen and near Sir Winston Churchill's picture, "Bottle-scape"

Mr. Lewis and Mrs. Min Lewis run a farm at Orchard House, Llanstephan, and this Academy picture shows a corner of the kitchen of Orchard House and immortalises a ham and a side of bacon produced and cured at Llanstephan. To say nothing of the eggs.

It is a striking picture which immediately catches the eye with its realism and perfect finish in the style of the early Flemish. It is a definite bit of Carmarthenshire with a typical Staffordshire china dog, inviting one to sit on the settee.

Newspaper Article 1950s

Oil Painting of Welsh Dresser
at Orchard House, Llanstephan, 1950s

FUNDS NEEDED

Sir - It is sad to think that the 13th century old Marbell Church in the Welsh Village of Llanybri is to be demolished because funds cannot be raised to restore it to its original beauty.

Situated on high ground and demanding attention in the centre of the village, it adds a medieval charm to the countryside. The rot has been allowed to develop over the last 17 years without shame by those responsible for its upkeep.

When gale force winds caused havoc to the roof of Laugharne Church, £5,000 was soon raised by the local people; if money cannot be found to restore the only historical building in Llanybri then the inhabitants should hang their heads in shame.

MIN LEWIS

Laugharne

He apparently married a wealthy lady who died giving birth to their only child, a girl, leaving all her possessions to her daughter. All went well for the girl until she came of age and fell in love with a gentleman from Carmarthen. Then the hangman, fearing that he would lose his wealth and no doubt his home, forbade her to see the gentleman again. To ensure that she would not elope, he imprisoned her in her own home by securing bars on the windows and locking the doors. Fearing that she might find a way of escaping the bolts and bars, he built a tiny room without windows in which to incarcerate her. Fortunately before the room was completed her lover rescued her from her prison and she eloped unharmed. The hangman's wrath drove him to despair, and in a fit of fury and a bout of melancholy he hanged himself.

The hangman died in 1905 and was buried at Llangynog church, but although I have searched the graveyard several times, I have failed to find his grave.

Carmarthenshire is principally a farming county, but Dylan's Uncle Jack was apparently not a good farmer.

A one-storied cottage was once a familiar sight in Wales, but now most of these cottages are ruins. An ancient right allowed villagers to erect a cottage on common land provided the house was built in a single night and that chimney smoke ascended from the chimney by morning. These were nicknamed 'one night houses' and were erected with stone and turf. Later, the turf was removed and a stronger material substituted: a yellow sticky plaster mixed with hair, straw and moss and pounded into a kind of mortar.

The early cottages were thatched, but later slate was used. The Welsh long house was the farmhouse and cowshed combined under one roof with only a partition wall dividing the domestic from the cows' residence. The exteriors of the houses were annually washed with white lime, and they still are in some places.

A farmer's wealth was reckoned by the size of the herd of cows he owned, the larger the herd, the richer the man, and the richer the man the greater the respect he demanded. Many of the farms have been handed down from father to son.

A Welsh kitchen conjures up the memory of an open dresser displaying blue plates and golden lustre jugs. Staffordshire dogs, a high wooden settle near an open fire, a scrubbed top table sometimes covered with oil-cloth. Cured hams and sides of bacon hanging from ceiling hooks, and a pot of cowl simmering on the fire. Cowl is a Welsh stew consisting of boiled bacon, leeks or onions and potatoes.

A round iron plank is used for cooking Welsh cakes and plank-bread. The fire is kept in continually by using pele. Pele is a mixture of coal dust and clay shaped into balls; these coal balls are so arranged that they sometimes burn for days without replenishing. This method of heating is cheap but extremely dusty.

Another Welsh delicacy is Layer-bread made from seaweed, it is a black and green colour. To cook, the layer-bread is coated with oatmeal and fried in hot bacon fat.

Dylan wrote in *Under Milk Wood:*

Second Drowned. Is there rum and laverbread?

The hospitality of the Welsh is renowned, and nowhere on earth could you be sure of a friendlier or kinder welcome. A meal is provided almost instantly with the best china and tablecloth used in honour of your visit, and usually an abundance of home-made cakes and tarts appear to tempt your appetite. Sometimes home-brewed beer or wine is produced for the guest to sample.

103

Dylan possessed much of this quality of generosity, for he was open-handed to the extreme. To him possessions meant nothing, and money was only a necessity to live.

When Dylan went to America, he asked the local shopkeepers to give Caitlin all the groceries she required for the family, while he was away. When he returned he immediately settled a bill of over £60, without dispute or quibble.

Memories from friends and neighbours:

Dylan's signature tune was 'The Day is Ended Little Drummer Boy', says Billy Williams, and he remembers singing it with Dylan on Swansea railway station on the way home, after seeing a cricket match there. They were joined by Dan Jones the musician, Alfred Janes the painter, and Ralf the books. Only the station staff objected to the rendering.

Dylan was drinking with Caitlin and a male friend about his own size. He laughed when the friend asked Caitlin to describe her idea of a perfect man.

'Tall, big and very handsome,' replied Caitlin.

'That just about describes us,' said Dylan with a twinkle in his eye.

The same friend once extolled Caitlin's beauty to Dylan.

'She's the most beautiful woman in Laugharne,' he said.

'No,' replied Dylan, 'I beg to differ. *Your wife* is the most beautiful woman in Laugharne.'

Dylan yearned for the day when he would no longer have to struggle for an existence. The years of borrowing and fear weighed heavily on his mind. Drink helped him forget the times between the cheques, when life did not seem at all rosy. A trip to America broke the monotony, bringing new faces, new ideas and money, the essential and sometimes the curse of mankind; the root of evil yet the necessity of life. How could a man live and dream in Laugharne without money?

What do the publicans of Laugharne remember of Dylan the villager and neighbour? 'Dylan was not the drinker people thought he was,' said Phil Richards of the Cross House Inn, where Dylan was a frequent but temperate visitor. 'He didn't know the value of money, but he certainly didn't die of drink.'

People of Laugharne were not overawed by the reputation of Dylan; he was essentially respected and regarded as a very likable person who had little effect, commercial or otherwise, upon the village.

Many villagers claim to know the originals of the characters in *Milk Wood*, and they do not seem to mind being used in this way at all. Well, there's a Polly Garter in every village like this, isn't there? In fact, it seemed quite a popular game for locals to spot likenesses between themselves and Dylan's characters.

In the churchyard, the small white wooden cross that marks Dylan's grave stands among larger more ostentatious marble headstones of better-kept graves. This grave, Dylan's house and the hut where he wrote are the tangible reminders of his association with Laugharne. The villagers seem slightly surprised at all the fuss.

Students are frequent visitors to Laugharne, as Swansea University College paper, *Crefft*, suggests. In their paper of January 1963, they devoted two middle pages to Memories of Dylan Thomas, written by four of his Swansea friends, under the title 'A Pubber of Genius'. This, for instance, by Sculptor Ronald Cour:

Before attempting to try and recapture something of my schooldays with Dylan

Llaregyb Players in Under Milk Wood, Laugharne

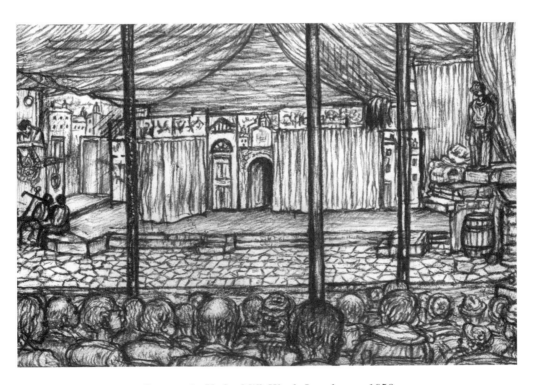

Stage set in Under Milk Wood, Laugharne, 1958

Pioneer Bus Passengers from Laugharne to Carmarthen

Thomas, it is very necessary to describe one or two aspects of the Grammar School as it was.

There were numerous practical jokers and 'ragging' was a daily feature. As far as the actual studies were concerned, the accent was very much on the sciences and the classics and very little enthusiasm existed for anyone who sought to engage in the arts. Consequently, Dylan who was dedicated to poetry and literature to the exclusion of almost all other subjects found himself hounded by the staff for his lack of appreciation of and dislike of engaging in any of the other subjects.

It is important to mention that Dylan's father-the great 'D.J.'-was senior English master at the school and it became abundantly clear that Dylan had the most superb background for his work, because it was a great thrill to hear the clarity and perfection of his father's amazing flow of the English language. Perhaps it would be true to say that the staff objected very much to the fact that Dylan managed to evade so effectively his duties in connection with the other subjects and this was indeed very much the case on his becoming assistant editor of the school magazine in 1929.

Dylan's interest in the arts was wide and varied and he appeared in school plays; as a matter of fact, he took the part of Oliver Cromwell in the production of that name.

He was, of course, a consistent contributor to the school magazine and there are many of his early poems published in the issues of the period.

He also submitted stories and articles, including one extremely interesting comment on 'The Films' which included references to aspects of the early work of that great producer, D. W. Griffith, and an account of the historical background to film making in this country. He was also responsible for publishing a very able article on a visit to an exhibition at Burlington House called 'Some characteristics of Persian Art'. In addition to this, he was keenly interested in music and the practice of the arts, and the Art Master revealed to me once that Dylan had consulted him and asked for a criticism on a piece of work which he had done in the 'abstract' idiom.

He was well liked by the boys and was always ready to join in the escapades such as returning quickly to the form room after a particular lesson in order to barricade the door with desks and resist the onslaught of the boys left outside-supported, of course, by the unheeded protestations of the Master concerned.

Another such plot, to be an active participant in the planning and execution of, involved the placing of a piece of cotton around the form room, supported by drawing pins and which held up the large picture of the village in the French lesson. The highlight of the whole carefully considered operation consisted of the cutting of the cotton in the middle of the hushed translation from one 'set book' or other, resulting in the rolled-up canvas picture unfurling with a mighty roar and great pandemonium. The cotton was attached to one of the desks in the front of the form room opposite the door. Dylan sat somewhere near the front opposite the door.

His amazing ability to enter wholeheartedly into the diverse activities of school life is typified by his entry for the Junior Mile in the School Sports and the result recorded in the magazine edition of July 1929 reads: One mile (under 15) 1st D. M. Thomas.

Alfred Janes, the painter, recalls early days in London:

In 1933, or thereabouts, Dylan came to live in London and shared a room with me in Redcliffe Street in South Kensington. I remember the journey well; my parents drove us up. Dylan, with one huge case, a pork-pie hat and an enormous check overcoat like a marquee over his slight frame. Our room, or studio, as it had become, since I had left the Academy and was painting on my own, seemed quite ordinary to me then, but when I think back on it now I am not surprised that it filled our parents, when they could steel themselves to visit us, with dismay. It was taken unfurnished, and from somewhere or other we had a couple of camp-beds, a table and an oven which looked like a biscuit tin and was placed over the gas ring. I was the chef but Dylan seldom seemed to eat; perhaps it was because my favourite dish was a huge pancake of boiled onions and potatoes fried afterwards to a golden brown; the colour I think meant less to him than it did to me! Later we were lent an iron bedstead which we found made an admirable wardrobe when placed up on end against the wall-castors out and covered with a sort of curtain. The only chair had been modified for use as an easel, so when we sat it was on the beds. I remember one of these collapsing completely under Dylan's father on one of his visits. This horrified me; after all, to me, Mr Thomas was still my erstwhile English master at the old school.

There must have been a strange contrast between us and our habits; whereas I was glued to my easel-cum-chair, experimenting day after day, Dylan would disappear for days-perhaps weeks-on end: on one occasion he went out to get a haircut and the next time I saw him was in Swansea months later; he'd been staying in Ireland somewhere!

He was undoubtedly tremendously restless, coming and going at all times.

Now a furious burst of work, often sitting up in bed with his hat and coat on to keep warm, then a complete disappearance from view only to turn up with some new friend-a down and out from the embankment-a broken-down American boxer- a Communist in hiding from Fascists after one of Mosley's meetings at Olympia- they would stay for a while, may be hours, days or weeks, then disappear for good.

During this period, we were joined by an old Swansea friend, Mervyn Levy, who was then at the Royal College of Art. We had some wonderful times together that have merged into a sort of kaleidoscopic image of laughter, arguments, theories, experiments, quarrels, gropings after more laughter; both Dylan and Mervyn could be enormously funny.

The poet Vernon Watkins has this to say of Dylan Thomas. He writes:

The title of Dylan Thomas's first American collection is *The World I Breathe*. It was taken from the poem in his second book, which begins with the line:
    'Today, this insect, and the world I breathe...
and ends
    'My cross tales behind the fabulous curtain.'
It was 1936 when this was written, a time when he was continually foretelling his own death and relating it to the dramatic stories, beginning with the story of Eden, which he saw projected by an unseen Creator. At this time, just as Heine used theatrical scenery to simplify his vision of the world, Dylan used film mechanism for his imagery. It is difficult to explain to anyone who did not know Dylan Thomas why any study of him must remain totally inadequate. It is equally difficult to explain why those who knew him find themselves deeply handicapped in writing about him.

The quality he prized most was seriousness and he was a born clown; but was there any other poet of recent times who could create so quickly an intimacy of judgement, an apprehension of what was valid in art and in life? That is perhaps one of the reasons why strangers who had met him only once for a long conversation felt after his death that they had known him all their lives.

The entertainer and the intellectual alike were slightly ashamed after meeting him, as he could beat them both at their own game; but if they were humble, they

108

Rough sketch idea of original bookcover
of Laugharne and Dylan Thomas

Milk delivery in Laugharne in the 1950's

Passengers in bus from Carmarthen to Laugharne

Brown's Hotel, Laugharne

quickly recognised that he was humble too. The prig was his *bête noir*, the pedant a black and white cross wood figure whom he didn't despise.

The variety of life and its abundance sang in his veins. He was born to praise it and he did so most completely when war distorted it into every manifestation of horror.

When the war ended, his own war continued. He was on the one hand, enriched by the heroic comedy of people's lives, for he loved people, and on the other, fascinated by artificial pattern, for the problems of form he had to solve in his last poems were subtler and more intricate than he had set himself before. He found freedom in the late broadcast scripts, but pattern obsessed him. In this late work, the prose, with all its humorous invention, was made by his social life, the poetry by his isolation in spite of that, the isolation of the entertainer who has taken off his mask.

A writer's mask can be fatal to him and it is certain that the image the age demanded of Dylan Thomas was accelerated by his popularity, his infectious humour deceived everyone but himself. His method was not to retreat from the mask hut to advance beyond it, and in that exaggeration remain completely himself.

He agreed readily with his detractors and did not at all mind being misunderstood. Then, in the private dark, his exuberance was subjected to the strictest control.

The public figure and the lyric poet, whose work began and ended in the Garden of Eden, came to terms, terms which no critic or friend has the complete equipment to analyse.

Of 'Dylan The Man' Mervyn Levy, the artist, has this to say:

Only a few people really knew Dylan Thomas. He had, of course, hundreds of acquaintances, many of whom, since his death, have claimed that they knew him. The mistake is not entirely one-sided. You can meet a congenial pubber only once and feel convinced at the end of the evening that you know the man, and Thomas was a pubber of genius, warm, generous, humorous, shedding his wit and delectable bawdiness with all the dazzling conviviality of the bubbles winking and bursting in a glass of lager. He could make any Tom or Dick feel that they really knew him. But they did not. The painter Alfred Janes, the composer Daniel Jones; the poet Vernon Watkins, these and a few more of his Swansea pals are the only people who can claim to have known him to the marrow of the lily bone.

He was, of course, as everyone knows, a drunkard whose days were shortened by his association with the scum of the American literary and bohemian scene, the puny poseurs who, in the words of a distinguished English writer, crawled over his flesh in the hope that they would thereby rub some of his fame on to themselves. He was, it is true, a spendthrift and a borrower, but not, as is popularly supposed, a practising wencher. He drank too much. Stupid women showered their money on him, but he cared for only one woman, ever-his wife, Caitlin. This he was not forgiven and so the stories of his infidelities abound. It is all malice.

In the last years of his life, he was ceaselessly bedevilled by a stream of rats who fed on the eggs of his reputation. Sucked at his generosity and finally nibbled away the very liver of his being, of these people, I will say no more. Brinnin has at least identified a number and Caitlin in her book *Leftover Life to Kill* has taken her revenge on the 'multitudinous, scavenging spawn of America' and on the 'matriarchs... indomitably avalanching to drain the reflex switches, and faint spasms, from the exhausted corpse'.

We shared many curious little cameos of experience when we were boys. I will recall just one. It occurred when we were around nine or ten years of age. My mother

111

died when I was eight, and after her death, my father engaged a succession of nurses to look after his three children. One of these was a particularly comely and buxom young girl whom Dylan and myself had long suspected of washing her breasts in the hand-basin. The glass panels of the bathroom door were masked with areas of variously coloured opaque paper, very thin and imparting to the top half of the door the aspect of a crude, stained glass window. One day, in the holidays, we carefully scraped away two minute peepholes, one on either side, in readiness for the view that we dreamed would confirm our delicious suspicions. And so, not long afterwards it turned out, around 3 p.m. we crept up the sleepy, dark, afternoon stairs and with an eye each to our respective peepholes, beheld in ecstasy, like two tiny elders, our own Susannah.

The last time I saw him was in the small hours, one night in 1948, when he arrived in Bristol without warning, in the battered car of a mutual friend. A furious battering around 1.30 a.m. was irritably attended by Mrs Musgrave, my landlady, and soon my own door was under fire.

'Mr Levy! Mr Levy! Quickly please! Some terrible men are asking for you!'

I tore into my trousers, pulled on a jacket and stumbled downstairs. In the hall stood Dylan, his hair matted in damp coils.

Against the open door, a light drizzle was falling. Tony Hubbard, his companion grinned a greeting at me from the driving seat of an ancient sports car. A crate of beer, many of the bottles already empty, occupied the whole of the back seat.

'Mervy,' said Dylan. 'We've come to see you.'

Wandering the streets of Bristol, we wove incredible fantasies as we so often did when we were together for a while. How many mice would it take to pull the London to Glasgow express? Half a million? A million? Oh! More, lots more! Don't forget, they'd have to pull it at the same speed as it normally goes. Anyway if you had enough mice, you could do it. It stood to reason. But you would have to lay special mouse-tracks (we discussed their character). And the mice, of course, would need egging-on. But how? Cats? No, they would make the mice hysterical. It would be essential to keep strict order. Well, then, thousands of midgets with whips stationed at intervals along the tracks? Yes, that seemed the most likely answer. Could you do it with worms? With five hundred billion of these struggling, squelching, loathsome creatures?

If you had enough, yes, obviously.

I saw little of Dylan in the last two or three years of his life. The last words he wrote to me were in a letter dated 1952. 'See you on the cross. Love Dylan'. Perhaps he will.

Dylan, of course, went to America of his own free will, being well paid for his performances. Had he been stronger willed he might have resisted the temptations of the social life that was showered upon him.

He was certainly unique, and the Americans loved him for it, and their enthusiasm for his work probably did more than the British to make his name world famous.

Dylan, having lived fifteen years in Laugharne, made many local friends who of course cannot claim and do not profess to claim to know him the same way as his Swansea intellectual friends.

They knew him as the man who drank with them in the pubs, they knew he was no ordinary man but they did not respect him as a poet because they did not understand his work. Tales of his escapades spread from one to another, and his witticisms were always good for a laugh.

112

Min Lewis in the Interior of Brown's Hotel

The Llaregyb Players in Under Milk Wood, Laugharne, 1958

Elwyn Samuel, secretary of the Carmarthen Community Council, once read an account in *The Times* announcing a reading that Dylan was expected to give to the Oxford Union. He was amazed to hear later, that Dylan quite unconcerned about the honour and the importance, forgot to turn up.

A year later, Dylan was again asked to make his appearance, and to make sure he would not forget the second time, the president of the Union drove to Laugharne to collect him.

Several months later, Elwyn again met Dylan in the Boars Head Hotel, Carmarthen, and as a means of conversation asked him how he had enjoyed reading to the Oxford Union.

'How do you know about that?' Dylan asked in surprise.

'I read it in *The Times*,' answered Elwyn.

'Well, to tell you the truth it was marvellous,' Dylan replied with a twinkle in his eyes. 'Do you know we had three hundred stops on the way!'

Another occasion, when Dylan and Elwyn met for a drink, they discussed the sudden death of a mutual friend.

'Oh well,' Dylan said. 'It was only to be expected, for she drank like a fish!'

Dylan liked to bet on horses, but he was not rash, according to Billy Williams, and he had tremendous fun studying form, especially laughing at the strange horses' names. It is not recalled whether he was a lucky gambler, but it is unlikely that he was.

Living one's life away in a Welsh village can be a monotonous existence, for besides the pubs there is no entertainment. No doubt it was imperative for Dylan to go to London occasionally to break the monotony of Laugharne.

There are people living in Wales today who have hardly been further than the village in which they were born, thus their outlook is narrow and often petty. But there are occasions which they look forward to with pleasure, the Cymanfa Ganu and the Eisteddfod.

Recent years have seen an increasing growth of Anglo-Welsh poets and writers, who are frowned on by the Eisteddfod and the Welsh Nationalists. Rhys Davies in his book *The Story of Wales*, wrote:

> Awareness of the nation has also spread by the recent and growing school of Anglo-Welsh writers who, while forsaking the old bardic traditions and the frequently parochial outlook, possess in their work a renewed and unmistakable flavour of their country. These writers of English are usually criticised as traitors by the Eisteddfod guardians and the stern Nationalists. Yet it is through them that knowledge of Wales filters into the world. This new school of writers has already begun a renaissance of national literature comparable to the Irish (Celtic) revival of some years ago (but less literary and wider in scope). Its members write; unselfishly, for all to read-in English, but the native flavour and spirit is there. Their brothers remain faithful to the Welsh language, are read widely on the right side of Offa's Dyke and also achieve admirable work in keeping the old language fresh and astute. In this domain, W. J. Gruffydd, its distinguished leader, makes scholarly efforts to keep a modern torch alight, notably in the magazine he edits, *Y Llennor.* Until the war suspended publication, the Anglo-Welsh school was able to run two magazines. *The Welsh Review,* edited by Gwyn Jones, a writer of distinction, and the scolding, rather impudent and lively little *Wales,* edited by the poet Keidrhych Rhys. Both these editors keep a fresh eye open for the new writers appearing daily on the horizon. The much discussed Dylan Thomas has fathered many of the new school of poets, though as yet none

achieves the long lovely ripples of his lines flowing on some golden unearthy beach full of legendary treasures. But Alun Lewis and Vernon Watkins possess the authentic fire, while the author of 'The Blue Bed,' Glyn Jones, seeks to express in fable and symbolic story the same surge of the rich new world they are discovering. There are others-like the guests at a wedding feast, too numerous to mention here.

One realises the truth of Rhys Davies's statement after reading Brinnin:

A further aspect of Dylan Thomas's poetry that appeals to Americans is the exotic unfamiliarity of its imagery. This is perhaps a lesser source of appeal, but an important one. While we think as a rule, of the exotic as something rarefied and out of reach and perhaps slightly bogus, the exotic in Dylan Thomas's poems is something that intrigues and charms us, because we have every confidence that he is giving us a vision of the world he sees and knows and that only by the accidents of time and place are we ourselves prevented from confirming the reality of his observations. It has been revealing to me for instance to recognise in Wales something I had known previously only as part of a poem.

A paragraph later he continues:

For years a particular image from one of Dylan Thomas's poems has always pleased me immensely, and that image is, 'the heron-priested shore'. To me, it has always conjured up a druidical series of tall birds standing as if in performance of some ritual along a water's edge. The picture I saw was large and quite pleasantly satisfying as a glimpse of far-away Wales. But since I had never actually seen a heron in its natural state, my experience of this image was, without my ever knowing it, quite vague and limited. But now that I have seen herons along the very shore where Thomas sees them, I am delighted to find that while my first impression has a literary validity, my new impression is based on the observations that herons do stand in sacerdotal attitudes, as if they were perpetually extending benedictions and that when they are surrounded by kittiwakes and oyster-catchers, they do recall priests crowded about by parishioners.

Then he goes on:

So that the point I want to make of my own experience is the fact that while so much of Dylan Thomas's world is strange to the American reader and shut away from observation; he has invested that world with such conviction and presented it so soundly that we accept his most exotic images with absolute confidence that they do not only grace the iconography of his poems but that they are generic to the landscape of his country.

Dylan was never known to bore his drinking companions with the serious side of his nature, for his work and his pleasure were worlds apart. To bring forth bellows of laughter from fellow drinkers, he often recited a nursery ditty, adding a naughty word to give it spice.

There was a f———— g spider crawled up the water spout,
Down came the rain and washed the F————r out,
Out came the sun and dried up the rain,
Then the f———— g spider went up the spout again.

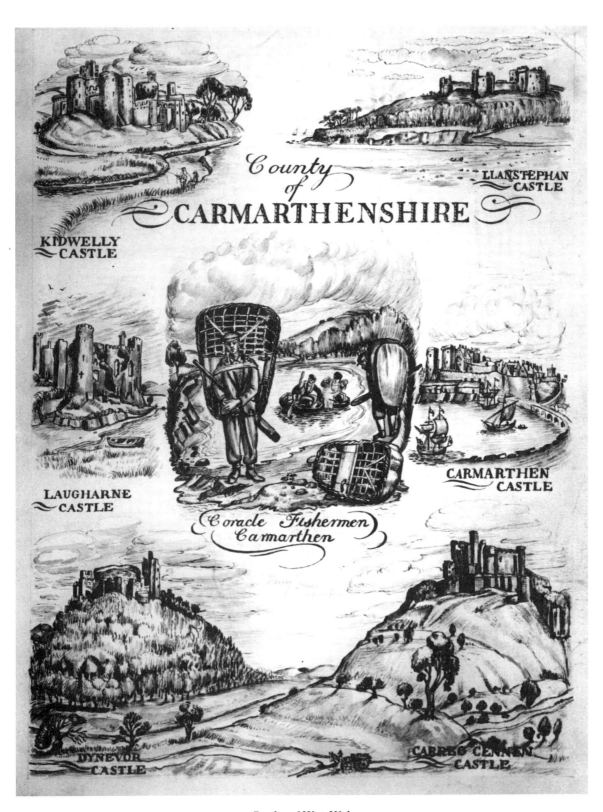

County
of
CARMARTHENSHIRE

LLANSTEPHAN
CASTLE

KIDWELLY
CASTLE

LAUGHARNE
CASTLE

Coracle Fishermen
Carmarthen

CARMARTHEN
CASTLE

DYNEVOR
CASTLE

CARREG CENNEN
CASTLE

Castles of West Wales

Portrait of Mr Billy Williams

'Buy a school burberry for Llewellyn,' was Caitlin's demand as he prepared to join Billy Williams on a trip to Carmarthen. 'But be sure to buy it from the "Best" outfitters.'

Off to town went Dylan in high spirits, and as they walked along Lammas Street, Dylan remembered the shopping he was asked to do.

'This shop is as good as any,' said Billy leading the way in. Dylan asked to be shown some burberrys, giving the age and the exact size of Llewellyn. One burberry they were shown was reasonably priced and the exact size required, but Dylan, remembering that he was supposed to go to the 'Best' outfitters, thanked the assistant for showing him the burberrys saying that he would view others before deciding. They then proceeded to the 'Best' outfitters, where Dylan was shown a burberry exactly the same as the previous one, except that it was two pounds dearer. Politely thanking the assistant, he declined to buy it and returned to the former outfitters to purchase the burberry he had first seen. Perhaps he was not as rash or as reckless with money as he was supposed to be.

Dylan, rather the worse for drink one evening after he had spent the day on a pub crawl with a London friend in a Jaguar car, called into a local pub for beer.

The night was rough with torrential rain, and the landlady charmingly greeted him in her 'Rolls-Royce' voice.

'Isn't it a dreadful night, Mr Thomas?' she asked.

Dylan hardly able to lift his pint, looked up, his eyes half-closed from stupor, and nodded, 'Yes,' he replied. 'It's f——g pissing outside.' Then he lowered his head to sip his beer again.

One day when there was a funeral in Laugharne, and some of the locals were discussing the virtues of the deceased in Brown's Hotel, Dylan turned to Billy Williams and said quite casually:

'I don't want a fuss made over me when I am dead, just bury me in the Green Banks; let there be no mournful faces grieving over me, I want everybody to be drunk at my funeral.'

POST-MORTEM

Finis Coronatopus, an appropriate Latin motto for the end of a book. 'The End Crowns All Work' and the end crowned Dylan's work and life. After many turbulent years of struggle, he was not laid in the Green Banks, under the castle walls where he had expressed a wish to be buried, but on a grassy slope away from the turmoil and bustle of life, where peace is only disturbed by woodpigeons flapping their wings in the branches of the trees, and the haunting cry of the curlews flying overhead, and the plaintive moos of cows being driven in to milk.

Gone is the St Bernard without any brandy, the Rolls-Royce selling fish and chips and Danny Raye. Gone is the poet who added colour to the Bible Black town; gone but not forgotten, for Dylan will always be a part of Laugharne as surely as the River Taf flows past the Boat House to the open sea.

Before he left Laugharne for the last time, he spoke of his fears to Mrs Billy Williams. 'I dread the trip to America,' he said seriously. 'The drinking is hard there, it's all raw spirit.'

Dylan was obviously a sensitive and shy man and it must have been a tremendous effort for him to appear before a large critical audience. Did he perhaps drink heavily so that he could forget himself and attain courage for the ordeal?

In England, the National Trust preserves the homes of famous authors. Bernard Shaw's house at Ayot St Lawrence, Hertfordshire, although off the beaten track, is frequently visited by strangers who admire his work. Rudyard Kipling's seventeenth-century Bateman's House, at Burwash in Sussex, Thomas Hardy's cottage at Higher Bockhampton, Dorchester, are in a sense, shrines. Thomas Carlyle's home in Cheyne Walk, Chelsea, is now a museum showing many of his possessions.

Beatrix Potter lived at Hill Top near Sawrey, Lancashire, and the house is furnished today as it was when she lived there. William Wordsworth's home at Cockermouth in Cumberland is preserved, as is the cottage at Nether Stowey on the Bridgwater-Minehead road, where Samual Taylor Coleridge lived.

Dylan Thomas's house remains as it was when he lived there, but it is locked against the intrusion of curious visitors. This is unfair to people who may come from countries as far distant as America because they are admirers of the poet and his work. Caitlin does not live there any more and the house is empty for ten or eleven months of the year. The damp mists, so frequent along the coast, are bound to damage the property in time, especially as it is not kept constantly heated.

The last film Dylan saw in Carmarthen was *Moulin Rouge.* The artist watching the artist; Toulouse Lautrec, painter, cripple, drunkard, respected because he was the son of a French count, with ample money to provide him with the necessities of life. His nights were spent in the Moulin Rouge with the noise, the women, the smoke and the drink. Night after night, he was there with an abundance of paper, sketching the acrobats, the can-can dancers, the musicians and the audience. Drinking absinthe and cognac in large quantities as he eagerly portrayed these colourful characters for posterity.

The drink helped him forget his deformed legs and aching body, giving him strength

120

THE
BOATHOUSE
PRIVATE

The Boat House, Laugharne

Thumbnail sketches of the stage set of Under Milk Wood, Laugharne, 1958

to face the world like a man. He sought company not with the aristocrats of France but with the drunkards and street-walkers, for they did not notice his crippled body, his money was as good as the rest.

Lautrec portrayed the life he enjoyed in his lithographic posters and paintings. He died after a life of heartbreaks, also a comparatively young man, but he did not die before leaving his mark in the world. He was a man with something to say and he said it.

Dylan was born in humbler circumstances, the son of middle-class parents, he was not a cripple neither was he rich, but like Lautrec he had tremendous battles to fight; it is certainly not easy trying to live an artist's life in Wales, where everything that does not conform to Welsh standards is criticised. He was dismissed as a curious fellow with peculiar habits, but like Lautrec he had the courage to live as he wished.

As Dylan watched the film on the life and death of Toulouse Lautrec, his own life too was drawing to an abrupt end, but unlike Lautrec who died in his familiar home, Dylan died on foreign soil, a stranger amongst strangers, who were as unfamiliar with his life as he was with theirs. During the film performance, Dylan suffered a blackout and was attended by a doctor.

The B.B.C. were recording a programme relating to Dylan from the Memorial Hall in Laugharne when Caitlin, who was amongst the audience, received the telegram informing her that Dylan was dangerously ill in an American hospital.

$$* \qquad * \qquad * \qquad *$$

Ever since 1957, an American couple, Fred and Viola Potgieter, have been making pilgrimages to Laugharne, seeking out people who knew Dylan a few of them embittered and embarrassed by his poetic sketches of them and tracing the landmarks he made famous.

Dylan Thomas was a man of excesses that were as boundless as his language was extravagant. But inch by inch, the Potgieters have covered the sombre Welsh countryside where he lived and worked. And through his intimates, they have discovered a man who was gentle, lovable, not in the least like the troublesome fellow portrayed in John Brinnin's *Dylan Thomas in America*. Viola Potgieter will confirm that Brinnin's account of Americans lionising the poet, feeding his ego, inflating him so there was no place left for him except an alcoholic dream world, has incised many a Welshman. And in their rejection, these Welsh friends tend to dismiss Dylan's own weaknesses and blame Brinnin for his role in arranging the lecture tour that the poet felt he needed and which brought his downfall.

'If that fellow would come to Laugharne, we'd run him out of town,' Billy Williams told Viola Potgieter at Brown's Hotel, which she describes as the community centre of friendliness for the town.

Fred and Viola Potgieter were our friends and guests when we lived at Laugharne. We met several years ago hardly by chance. A Dylan Thomas fan since 1948, Viola Potgieter simply knocked on our door to ask about the poet, and that, according to Viola, was when his living world began to open for the Potgieters.

'Light breaks where no sun shines,' the poet wrote. And he might have been describing the 1958 encounter when the Potgieters entered our home.

A Dylan Thomas festival is a three-yearly event in Laugharne. In 1961, his poetic drama, *Under Milk Wood,* was presented in five performances at Wooford Theatre, by the Llaregyb Players.

Viola Potgieter describes a comment overheard as she sat in the darkened marquee.

'They know Dylan will be here. That's those empty seats in the front row. They are for Dylan, his father and his mother,' a voice behind her said.

'1 could believe this. The love for Dylan and of Dylan is a tangible thing there as well as with us who read and re-read and try to remember his golden voice, a Welsh singer of poems,' Mrs Potgieter recounts.

What did the poet think of his friends in Laugharne? He has written of them:

> That though I loved them for their faults,
> As much as for their good,
> My friends were enemies on stilts,
> And their heads in a cunning cloud.

Cliff Walk? The Boat House where Dylan and Caitlin Thomas lived out their turbulent marriage? Sir John's Hill, Fern Hill?

These landmarks were visited in conversation as frequently as they were visited in fact. And the graveyard too, where the poet lies beneath a painted pine cross.

'I was appalled at the state of the grave and at the wooden marker,' says Viola Potgieter and said so to her husband.

'Did the pine monument take you to Laugharne or his works?' her husband answered. In his book *Quite Early One Morning*, Dylan describes a visit to America:

He is vigorously welcomed at the station by an earnest crew art platoon of giant collegiates, all chasing the butterfly Culture with net, notebook, poison bottle, pin and label, each with at least thirty-six terribly white teeth, and is nursed away, as heavily gently as though he were an imbecile rich aunt with a short prospect of life, into a motor-car in which for a mere fifty miles or so travelled at poet breaking speed, he assures them of the correctness of their assumption that he is half-witted by stammering inconsequential answers in an over-British accent to their genial questions about what international conference Stephen Spender might be attending at the moment or the reactions of the British poets to the work of a famous American whose name he did not know or catch. He is then taken to a small party of only a few hundred people, all of whom hold the belief that what a visiting lecturer needs before he trips on to the platform is just enough martinis so that he can trip off the platform as well. And, clutching his explosive glass, he is seen contemptuously dismissing in a flush of ignorance and fluency, the poetry of those androgynous literary ladies with three names who produce a kind of verbal extoplasm to order as a waiter dishes up spaghetti. Only to find that the fiercest of these, a wealthy huntress of small seedy lions (such as himself) who stalks the middle-western bush with ears and rifle cocked, is his hostess for the evening. Of the lecture, he remembers little, but the applause .and maybe two questions. 'Is it true that the English intellectuals are really psychological?' or 'I always carry Kierkegaard in my pocket. What do you carry?'

Late at night, in his room, he fills a page of his journal with a confused, but scathing, account of his first engagement; summarises American advanced education in a paragraph that will be meaningless tomorrow and falls to sleep where he is immediately chased through long, dark thickets by a Mrs Mabel Frankincense McHaffey, with a tray of martinis and lyrics.

And there goes the other happy poet bedraggledly back to New York which struck him all of a sheepish never-sleeping heap at first but which seems to him now, after the ulcerous rigours of a lecturer's spring, a haven cosy as toast, cool as an icebox and safe as skyscrapers.

Laugharne was home to Dylan, where he was a familiar sight walking along the cliff to the Boat House, with a jar of pickled onions in one pocket and a bottle of beer in the other, his short coat sagging wearily with the weight.

Laugharne was the place where they expected him to look and live like everyone else, no better, no worse, no richer, no poorer. What they could not understand was not worth bothering with anyway.

'Gosport Cats, Stoneyway Rats, and Upstreet Lords and Ladies,' sang the ghosts of the past, as the cherry trees in King Street downed fresh green leaves and blushed pink flowers in the spring sunshine.

The cuckoo's blatant voice echoed across the green hills and spinneys, and boys shouted to each other as they chased a ball across Cors field.

Along the Cliff Walk, small girls in gaily patterned dresses picked the primroses and dog violets that hid shyly behind leaves and tall grasses.

Young lovers linked arms, strolled, mumbled words of sweet endearment to one another and carved their initials, bold and strong on the wooden seat. Somebody wrote a girl's measurements in chalk on the blue door of Dylan's work-shed. 'Agatha Light, 34-23-34', not yet a Mae West, but the years bring forth an increase!

Sir John's Hill, awakened after a long winter sleep, wore a fresh mantle of green as it watched the small rowing-boats bobbing like corks on the ever restless water. Curlews, cormorants, herons, gulls and teal watched the incoming tide. Watching, listening, hearing! Expecting dabs, millet, shrimps and bass, alive so very much alive after a winter of solid ice that covered the bay like a rink, so that the Llanstephan hill shivered under a mantle of snow.

The hard breath of winter was already forgotten in the warm spring sunshine. Forgotten were the burst pipes and snowbound roads, the red sniffling noses and the chilblained feet, the North wind whining down the tall chimneys like a wailing banshee and the endless hunger of a starving fire.

It was ten years since they brought Dylan back to Laugharne for the last time, ten years and a couple of months, and the Boat House, sad and lonely, stared wide eyed at a path the zigzag path that rose like a wriggling worm to the locked gate.

'Hullo,' I said, but the house did not answer, for I was just another stranger staring at its shabbiness, sorry for its loneliness. Perhaps it did not know, how could it know, that I was enquiring after a poet who left full of hope, never to return?

There, on the belly of the cliff it stood, tucked away below a bank of sandstone rock as if it was ashamed to be seen.

What tales you could tell of the poet who favoured dabs and daps and sockless feet, who wore misshaped clothes with pockets bulging pickled onions and bottled beer. Instead, you stand like a mute, seeing all, hearing all but saying nothing.

Slowly I retraced my steps and met an old man with bloodshot eyes and grey clipped hair beheath a greasy cloth cap, clipping the hedge and dreaming of his long lost youth. He paused as I passed, and sucked the stem of an unlit pipe.

'It's cold for the time of year,' he said. 'The cuckoo was late this spring; there's no sign of Pembroke potatoes; the women are waiting to go to Stackpool, they are buggers for punishment!'

'Do you remember Dylan Thomas?' I asked.

'Aye, I remember 'im well enough, he was an ordinary bloke, kept to hisself a lot, never spoke much to anybody. Looked more like a tramp than a poet, he liked his beer before dinner and after, and always 'ad a fag dangling from his mouth. He was 'armless as far as I could see, never did no one no 'arm.'

'Did you ever join him for a drink?'

The old man eyed me suspiciously. 'Well, not joined 'im exactly, I met 'im at the Brown's and at the Cross sometimes, he always seemed a quiet man, never spoke much to anyone and never against 'em.'

'Do many strangers come to Laugharne because of Dylan Thomas?'

He rubbed his neck where the rough Welsh flannel shirt irritated the skin, 'Well, I suppose they do, but Laugharne was 'ere before Dylan Thomas so I can't see what all the fuss is about.'

As I thanked him for the chat, he laughed, spat on his hands and resumed his mechanical movement with the clippers.

I turned the bend and passed a yard where tall graves marked the last resting places of Hannah, Mary, John, Thomas, Blodwen, Myfanwy and Idris Jones. The graveyard of the Congregational chapel that had long disappeared. Tall grasses covered the mounds of earth, but here and there wild flowers peeped from the grass and life flourished amongst the dead.

A dog, startled by my sudden appearance, barked a warning and edged nervously away. A door of a house in Victoria Street opened as two small girls ran into the street, skipped along the pavement and hopped out of sight. A man with a small home-made wooden trolley delivered milk as if he had been doing it before the world began.

Sea View, the tall, gaunt house that was Dylan's second home, had aged with the years and the weather, and gaping roof holes stared into the sky and prayed that rain would not fall to rot its timbers. Even the chimneys seemed ready to topple at a mere breath of wind.

The window that had once crushed the poet's hands was closed and as blind as Captain Cat, as I leaned on the wall to stare more closely at the house.

'Hullo,' I said, but the house did not answer. 'Do you remember the poet who was young and full of hope, he had a wife and a child when he lived with you? He drank beer and looked across at the bay when he wrote, he was thin and in love with life, but he left a long time ago.'

At Mariner's Corner, a group of small children stood smiling and sucking ice blues. 'Do you know who Dylan Thomas was?' I asked.

But how could I blame them if they did not know, was he not dead before they were born?

It was ten long years since they brought him back to Laugharne, back to the tall house called the Pelican in the main King Street.

Dylan's mother, when she was bedridden, saw him going into the Brown's Hotel everyday. 'Oh, that I could see him coming out!' she would exclaim, but it was always dark when he came out; bible black dark in the small Welsh town. We shall never see him going in or coming out again.

126

Dylan's second home in Laugharne, Sea View

Portrait of Dylan Thomas

The bar of the Brown's is unchanged, there is a long seat beneath the bay window where Dylan sat and watched the people 'slowly, dopily, wandering up and down the streets like Welsh opium-eaters, half asleep in a heavy bewildered daze.'

There is a skittle board and a dart board, round tables and hard chairs, and a photograph of Dylan and Caitlin hanging on the wall.

It was in this bar that many locals sat one Saturday, while Jack Howells made his film about Dylan Thomas. We laughed and drank, joked and peered curiously at the camera, it seemed an endless job.

But Laugharne lives on, windswept and rainsoaked, chilled by easterly winds and scorched by the summer sun, bright with cherry trees, studded with cobblestones, up hill and down dale, with one portreeve, one recorder, burgresses and common land. Cockles, curlews, crosses, cusses, dolls, dames and demons, mud banks and yellow sand.

Once they fought like pirates down street, while up street toffs twittered and trembled in their well-polished shoes.

Along Featherbed Lane, the birds are making love as tongue-ferns hungrily sip the dew that falls in the spring evening.

Cows low in East Hill fields as women gather in groups to gossip.

'Who drank too much beer in the Farmer's Arms?'

'Who is going to have a baby?'

'Who is dead?'

'Anniversary in the chapel.'

'Paternity cases at court.'

'Babies up the chimneys.'

'Kisses behind the door.'

'Percy Ship's gone to sea.'

'Who was Dylan Thomas?'

This black magical town proud to speak English, knowing little Welsh, sleeps in the twilight hours and awakes refreshed to begin again.

LIST OF WRITINGS QUOTED

The page reference in parenthesis is to the book cited. Other numbers refer to the page in this book on which a quotation appears.

Bradley, A. G., *Highways and Byways in South Wales* (Macmillan & Co Ltd, London 1898) 45

Brinnin, John M., *Dylan Thomas in America* (J. M. Dent & Sons Ltd, London 1956) 79 (86), 116 (99-100)

Cour, Ronald; Alfred Janes; Mervyn Levy; Vernon Watkins; 'A Pubber of Genius' in *Crefft* (Swansea University College, January 1963) 104-112

Curtis, Mary, *The Antiquities of Laugharne, Pendine and their Neighbours* (R. Clay, Sons & Taylor, London 1880) 25, 26, 29, 30, 38, 41, 42, 49, 53, 61, 80

Davies, Rhys, *The Story of Wales* (Win. Collins Sons & Co Ltd, London 1943) 34, 115

Jones, Jim, Programme for the second production of *Under Milk Wood* at Laugharne, 1961 77-78

Parry Jones, D., *Welsh Country Upbringing* (B. T. Batsford Ltd, London 1948) 33, 38

Rhys, Keidrhych, Programme for the first production of *Under Milk Wood*, 18th August, 1958 73-74

Thomas, Dylan, *Collected Poems* (J. M. Dent & Sons Ltd, London 1952) 123 (24), 124 (107)

—— *Portrait of the Artist as a Young Dog* (J. M. Dent & Sons Ltd, London 1940) 33-34 (13-14), 100 (9-10)

—— *Quite Early One Morning* (J. M. Dent & Sons Ltd, London 1954) 29-30 (71), 50 (71), 87 (17), 92 (19), 124-125 (68-69)

—— *Under Milk Wood* (J. M. Dent & Sons Ltd, London 1954) 50 (42), 53(23), 83 (69), 103 (5)

Vale, Edmund, *How to See England* (B. T. Batsford Ltd, London 1937) 61

Thumbnail Sketches of Characters in 'Under Milk Wood'

Thumbnail Sketches of Characters in 'Under Milk Wood'

Thumbnail Sketches of Characters in 'Under Milk Wood'

Thumbnail Sketches of Characters in 'Under Milk Wood'

Sketch Portrait of Captain Cat - Llaregyb Player, 1958

Portrait of Min Lewis

Self Portrait of Stanley Lewis and Portrait of his mother

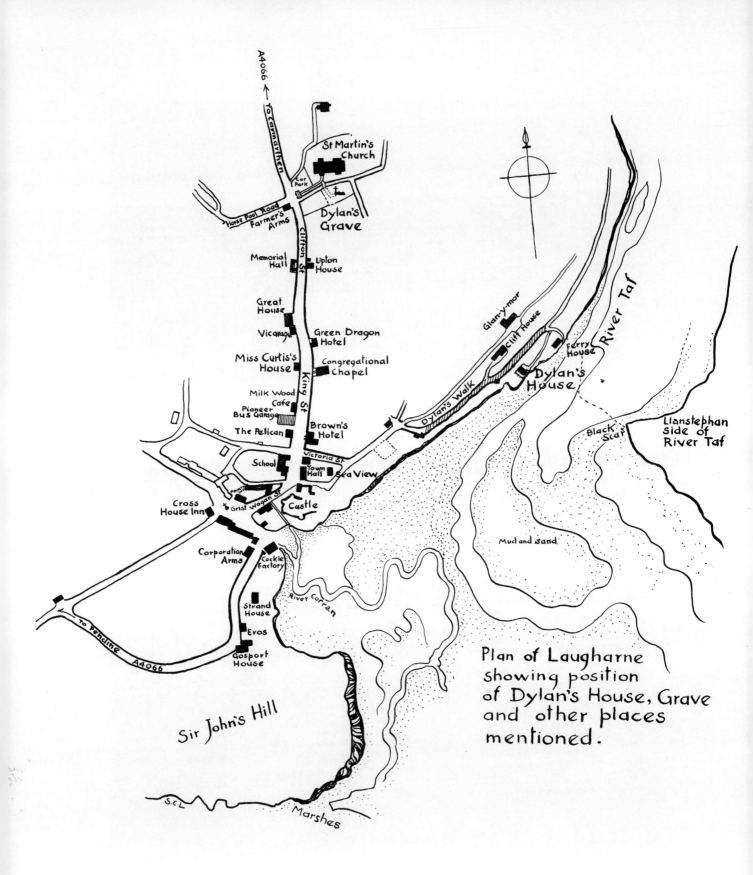

Plan of Laugharne showing position of Dylan's House, Grave and some of the other places mentioned

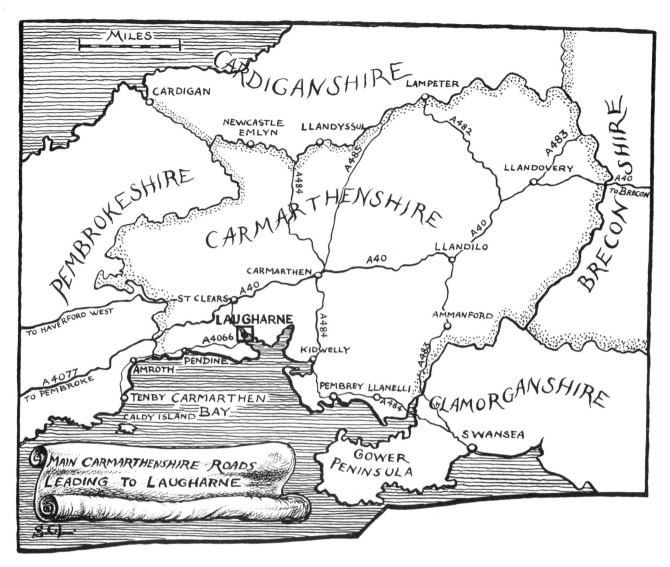

Welsh Dragon

FOR THE CHILDREN

THE ARTISTIC TURKEY

—By— MIN LEWIS

THERE Was one time of the year that Tommy Turkey hated more than any other; that was Christmas time. So many of his ancestors had been slaughtered at that period that each Christmas Turkey felt so sad that he went hiding in a thick wood at the back of the farm.

Christmas was coming. He could hear the children singing carols. Turkey had a tingling feeling and his face was very red; his brothers and sisters were quite concerned and tried to cheer him up.

"Farmer gives us extra corn before Christmas," smiled Teena Turkey.

"I know why," replied Turkey miserably. "So that we grow fat to sell in the market."

Because of he snow the farmer would not let the turkeys out, so there was no way for Tommy to escape. He sat miserably on the perch and refused to eat.

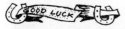

The other turkeys gobbled happily, they were so stupid that they did not realise why they were fed so well.

The farmer caught the turkeys one by one to take to market, they were put in crates with no room to move. Tommy was cramped and uneasy, the tears fell down his cheek and damped his spirit.

It was a long ride to market, the tractor chugged and puffed uphill. Tommy thought the earth looked very beautiful, he longed to fly to the top of the tall pine trees and look down on the world, for he felt he was born to nobler things.

At last he saw the lights of the town.

"Dump 'em 'ere," sad a loud uncouth voice, and the farmer unloaded the turkeys among bunches of prickly holly and Christmas trees. Tommy Turkey thought it all undignified and uncomfortable.

Presently butchers with blue and white striped aprons and straw hats began feeling the turkeys' breasts.

One fat butcher with a black moustache opened the crate to get a better look, this was the opportunity that Tommy was waiting for. He pushed passed the other turkeys and flew around the market. There was a terrible commotion. He knocked over trays of oranges and mixed nuts, people ducked as he flew over as if they expected him to drop a bomb.

A woman with a shrill voice threw a long stick at him, but it missed Tommy and broke one of the light bulbs. At last Tommy saw the opendoor and flew out into the fresh, freezing air.

On and on he flew far from the maddening cries of the market people and eventually flew into an artist's shop. There were canvases and tubes of paints and the strong smell of turps and linseed oil. Turkey trod on a pallet covered with coloured oil paints and from that he flew onto a clean white canvas. He made a most interesting pattern, and was so pleased with his work that he flew onto the pallet again and then back to the canvas.

The canvas began to take shape : the reds blended with the blues and the yellows with the greens. The pattern was exquisite.

The owner of the shop was Monsieur Alfonse, who was thinking of selling the shop because he made little money, hardly enough to pay the rates.

When he heard the confusion in his shop he hurried in. When he saw Turkey's picture he rubbed his eyes.

"What genius has been at work in my shop?" he asked. "Such beauty, such exquisite colour, such pattern." When he saw Turkey he said, "My beautiful bird you are the king of all birds for you have created a masterpiece."

On Christmas Day, Tommy Turkey sat near a yule log fire and feasted on Christmas pudding and cake crumbs. Alfonse refused to cook the turkey he had bought and gave it to a poor family in town - he dared not insult his guest.

Boxing Day dawned chill and dull. Tommy Turkey tucked his head under his wing and slept until he was suddenly awakened by Monsieur Alfonse.

"Mon beau Turkey, my precious one, my genius, the press are here, they want to take your photograph."

When the cameras flashed tommy was frightened. He got up and flew round and round the room knocking down canvases and tubes of paint.

Tommy Turkey slipped on the pallet of paint and landed on a clean canvas and a picture began to take shape.

"Out," shouted Alfonse to the reporters. "My Turkey is temperamental; he is at work on a masterpiece again."

When the reporters had gone and the room was quiet, Turkey perched on the canvas and slept; his masterpiece was finished.

Monsieur Alfonse stroked Turkey's feathers lovingly, "My beauty, my exquisite one," he murmured. "Your painting shall be exhibited in the great galleries of London and then Paris."

The critics raved over them, art magazines published coloured photographs, and cultured Sunday newspapers devoted a whole page to him.

An American millionaire bought the paintings for thousands of pounds and Alfonse sold his art shop and bought a fashionable house in London. Turkey now lived in complete luxury and slept on pure silk cushions embroidered in gold thread.

He grew fat and contented and had no fear of Christmas again, and when he became rich his genius left him and he never painted a masterpiece again.

WESTERN MAIL
MONDAY, FEBRUARY 26, 1962

ABSTRACTS

SIR - Mr. Shapiro states in his letter that there are many opportunities for both abstract and realistically inclined painters to exhibit in various exhibitions throughout the country, and I noticed particularly how he cautiously put in brackets, the British Isles. He knows only too well that all the contemporary Welsh exhibitions are dominated by abstractions.

It is assumed that abstraction is akin to music, yet whereas Welsh music like Spanish, German or French music is a characteristic of the individual country, abstract art is akin to no country. It has become an international means of expression, a balderdash style that has travelled like a steam-roller flattening the individual characteristics of every country of the world, until the great traditions of the past have been melted down into an indistinguishable style.

It is obvious to the most untutored observer of these pictures that abstraction is a regimented style. It has always been accepted that an artist is an individualist, therefore have modern artists lost courage, faith and above all their way?

Victor Pasmore, Ceri Richards and Jackson Pollock, as Mr. Shapiro states, are some of the leading abstract painters of the day, but it is an assumption to think that everyone must enjoy and be enthralled by their works, and by their aping followers, for these artists only fill a very minute corner of the world of art.

Unfortunately abstract art has not only become a cult, but a cuckoo in the nest as well, and we have lost all sense of proportion.

MIN LEWIS.

Laugharne.

Min Lewis was a prolific writer practically all her life and wrote hundreds of stories for children. A vast amount of them were printed regularly in the South Wales Evening Post in the 1950's and 1960s and Stanley Lewis illustrated all.

Tributes paid as author dies

SADNESS surrounds this week's civic celebrations in Newport to mark its new city status, following the sudden death of Kington author Min Lewis.

Min, who was invited to Newport with her artist husband Stanley as special guests of honour, died at her home in Church Street this week.

The couple, who during their busy lives together knew Dylan Thomas and his wife, Caitlin, had recently been the subject of much media attention.

This was because of Stanley's wartime painting which has become a focal point of Newport's pride.

Canvas

In the early stages of the war, Stanley, who was head of the art department at Newport College, used a large canvas to portray local figures involved in the war effort.

For many years, the paintings had been rolled up and put away, but it has since caused huge interest in Newport where it is now part of the new city display.

Min has written a series of highly popular children's books, all beautifully illustrated by her husband, a frequent Royal Academy contributor.

She also wrote a biography of Dylan Thomas, having known him and his wife during the time she and Stanley lived in Laugharne.

Min also collaborated with Arnold Haskell on a book about children's antiques.

By Sally Boyce

"Sometimes a mysterious greyness hides the green patchwork hills across the river; it is still and peaceful except for the cries of curlews and screeching gulls. When the day is clear a heron can be seen fishing in the pools, hunting flat fish in the sandy mud. Sometimes a boat bobs on the restless moving water, sometimes a stranger with a camera will try to capture the mysterious beauty, and look enraptured at the small cottage Boat House, and see Sir John's Hill, and hear a hundred, no a thousand voices cry out, 'This is Laugharne', for this is surely Laugharne and this was Dylan's home."

-extract from an article by Min Lewis in the current issue of

Country Quest

The magazine for Wales and the Border. On sale at bookstalls, newsagents, or from Caxton Press, Oswestry, Salop
Price 2/6

Min Lewis b. 1919 - d. 2003